Tort Law in Mauritius

Tort Law in Mauritius

Goran Georgijevic

Jonas Knetsch

This book was originally published as a monograph in the International Encyclopaedia of Laws/Tort Law.

Founding Editor: Roger Blanpain
General Editor: Frank Hendrickx
Volume Editor: Britt Weyts

Wolters Kluwer

Published by:
Kluwer Law International B.V.
PO Box 316
2400 AH Alphen aan den Rijn
The Netherlands
E-mail: lrs-sales@wolterskluwer.com
Website: www.wolterskluwer.com/en/solutions/kluwerlawinternational

Sold and distributed by:
Wolters Kluwer Legal & Regulatory U.S.
920 Links Avenue
Landisville, PA 17538
United States of America
E-mail: customer.service@wolterskluwer.com

ISBN 978-94-035-1029-3

e-Book: ISBN 978-94-035-1039-2
web-PDF: ISBN 978-94-035-1049-1

The Authors

Goran Georgijevic, a Mauritian citizen, was born in Smederevo (Serbia) in 1979. Before he completed his PhD in Comparative Contract Law and his LLM at the University of Bordeaux (France), he had graduated from the Faculty of Law in Belgrade (Serbia).

He is currently Senior Lecturer (Civil Law) at the Faculty of Law and Management of the University of Mauritius, where he held the position of Lecturer from August 2019 to February 2023. Before joining the University, he had been working for the Law Reform Commission of Mauritius (2012–2021).

He has published three books and more than a dozen peer-reviewed papers on Mauritian Civil Law.

Jonas Knetsch was born in Berlin (Germany) in 1982. Before his PhD in Comparative Tort Law, he graduated from the University Panthéon-Assas (Paris, France) and the University of Cologne (Germany).

From 2013 to 2017, he held a professorship at the University of Reunion Island, where he was largely involved in developing international relations with universities in the Comoros, Madagascar, Mauritius and Mozambique. He is currently a Professor at the Sorbonne Law School (University Paris 1 Panthéon-Sorbonne).

He has published extensively in tort and insurance law as well as in comparative law. He is an elected member of the International Academy of Comparative Law and of the European Centre of Tort and Insurance law (ECTIL) in Vienna. Lately, he has conducted research projects on tort law and insurance law issues related to data protection, personal injury and self-driving cars, as well as on the interplay of social security, private insurance, and tort law compensation.

The Authors

Table of Contents

List of Abbreviations

Ass plén	Assemblée plénière (*Full Court of the French Court of Cassation*)
Bull	Bulletin de la Cour de cassation (*Information Bulletin of the French Court of Cassation*)
Cass	Cour de cassation (*French Court of Cassation*)
CE	Conseil d'État (*French State Council*)
CILSA	Comparative and International Law Journal of Southern Africa
Civ	Chambre civile (*Civil Chamber of the French Court of Cassation*, until 1947)
Civ 1/2/3	1ère/ 2e/ 3e chambre civile (*First, Second, Third Civil Chamber of the Court of Cassation*)
Com	Chambre commerciale (*Commercial Chamber of the Court of Cassation*)
Crim	Chambre criminelle (*Criminal Chamber of the Court of Cassation*)
CUP	Cambridge University Press
D	Recueil Dalloz
ICLQ	International & Comparative Law Quarterly
JETL	Journal of European Tort Law
LGDJ	Librairie Générale de Droit et de Jurisprudence
MR	Mauritius Report
OJLS	Oxford Journal of Legal Studies
OUP	Oxford University Press
Req	Chambre des requêtes (*Chamber of Petitions of the Court of Cassation*, until 1947)
RIDC	Revue Internationale de Droit Comparé
SCJ	Supreme Court Judgment
UKPC	Judicial Committee of the Privy Council

List of Abbreviations

Preface

This monograph is intended to give a comprehensive and detailed overview of the tort law of Mauritius, which is the result of a legal *métissage*, reflecting the multiethnic, multicultural and multilingual character of the Mauritian society. While the civil law is still under a strong influence of the French codification, the gradual affirmation of a genuine legal identity and the hybrid character of the case law, drafted in English but often referring to French legal sources, put the law of Mauritius in a unique position among mixed legal jurisdictions.

Our book includes information relevant to practitioners, students and legal researchers in Mauritius and other parts of the world. It is aimed at everyone who is curious about the historical and current developments of the Mauritian tort law system. Particular attention has been given to references to the case law of the Supreme Court of Mauritius as well as to the relevant legal literature.

Another goal of our research is to add a contribution to legal scholarship on the law of the Indian Ocean, which still remains on the sidelines of the major publishing houses. We therefore express our gratitude to Wolters Kluwer and to our colleague Britt Weyts (University of Antwerp) for having accepted the publication of this monograph, dedicated to a 'small jurisdiction', in the prestigious International Encyclopaedia of Laws. Our thanks also go to Margot Leysen for the editorial coordination and her unfailing patience.

Jonas Knetsch wrote the General Introduction, Part III (Chapters 2 to 6) and Part IV (Chapters 1 and 2). Goran Georgijevic wrote Part I, Part II, Part III (Chapter 1), Part IV (Chapters 3 and 4), Part V and Part VI.

Paris (France) and Moka (Mauritius), December 2023

General Introduction

§1. General Background of the Country

I. Geography

1. The Republic of Mauritius is an island nation in the Indian Ocean, constituted of Mauritius Island and several outlying islands. Mauritius Island is located 2,000 km off the southeast coast of Africa and, together with Réunion (a French overseas department), forms part of the Mascarene Islands. While Mauritius is one of the world's smallest countries with a total land size of 2,040 km^2 and a population of 1.265 million people (as of 2019), its exclusive economic zone of 1.285 million km^2 is one of the twenty-five largest in the world.

2. Mauritius Island is 65 km long and 45 km wide and lies about 800 km east of Madagascar. As all other Mascarene Islands, it is of volcanic origin and surrounded by sandy beaches and coral reefs. The island's landscape consists of a coastal plain in the northern part, rising to a central plateau bordered by small mountains. The highest point of the island is Piton de la Petite Rivière (828 m). More than half of the island is arable; it is almost entirely planted in sugarcane, with vegetables, fruits and tea for local consumption also being grown. The climate is maritime subtropical, with temperatures varying from 25 degrees at sea level to the upper 10s on the high plateau. There is a warm, dry winter from May to November and a hot, wet and humid summer the remaining time.

3. The island of Mauritius is subdivided into nine districts (Flacq, Grand Port, Moka, Pamplemousses, Plaines Wilhems, Port Louis, Rivière du Rempart, Rivière Noire and Savanne), consisting of one city, four towns and 130 villages. The most populated municipality is Port Louis (146,000 inhabitants) which is also the capital city of the Republic of Mauritius and the country's economic and political centre. It is administered by the Municipal City Council of Port Louis.

4. The State of Mauritius is also composed of the island of Rodrigues and some smaller outlying islands. Rodrigues is situated about 550 km to the east of Mauritius Island, with a population of about 42,000, mostly of African descent. Its economy is based on fishing, farming, handicrafts and, more importantly, a developing tourism sector. The island gained autonomous status in 2002 and is governed by the Rodrigues Regional Assembly, situated in Port Mathurin, the administrative and economic centre of the island.[1] Among the Outer Islands of Mauritius, mention should also be made of Agaléga, two isolated islands situated 1,000 km to the north of Mauritius Island and with a population of 300, and of the Chagos Archipelago, constituted as the British Indian Ocean Territory at the time of independence and since then claimed as Mauritian territory.

II. History

A. *From the Discovery of Mauritius Island to the Arrival of the Dutch East India Company*

5. The Indian Ocean was known to Ancient Greece, but it was probably not until the development of the Arabo-Indian naval trade that the island of Mauritius, uninhabited until then, was discovered by Arab seafarers during the tenth century or even earlier.[2] Yet, historians do not rule out the possibility of an accidental discovery of the island, for example, by sailors of Ancient India before the island became known to the Arabs. In any case, the islands of Mauritius and Rodrigues appear on an Italian map produced in 1502 under their Arabic names, Dina Arobi and Dina Maroze. Despite this historical evidence of the Arabs' discovery of Mauritius, there is no trace left of their passage.

6. As the Arabs shared their vast geographical knowledge with their neighbours, European merchants took an interest in the Indian Ocean from the fifteenth century on. With the discovery of a sea route round the Cape of Good Hope, the Portuguese rediscovered and visited Mauritius and the surrounding islands (Reunion, Rodrigues), named the Mascarene Islands after the Portuguese explorer Pedro Mascarenhas. The Portuguese, however, took no interest in the isolated islands and, being already established in Mozambique, Goa (India) and on the Malaysian coast, did not consider a permanent settlement in a place where no precious stones, spices, silk or other riches could be found.

7. With the rise of the Dutch Republic as an important European political power, an increasing number of fleets were sent out by Dutch merchants to compete in the intercontinental spice trade, leading to the foundation of the Dutch East India Company. In 1598, a fleet of eight ships ran into a violent tempest while passing the Cape of Good Hope. Five ships from the fleet managed to reach the island of Mauritius. They landed and decided to name the island 'Mauritius' after Prince Maurits of the

1. On this topic, *see* André Oraison, *L'avènement d'un régime d'autonomie interne à Rodrigues dans le cadre d'un État mauricien unitaire*, 59 Revue juridique et politique des États francophones 78–96 (2005).
2. For a comprehensive survey of the history of Mauritius, *see* in particular Sydney Selvon, *A New Comprehensive History of Mauritius* (M. DS Editions, 2nd ed. 2018, 2 vol.); Megan Vaughan, *Creating the Creole Island: Slavery in Eighteenth-Century Mauritius* (Duke University Press 2005). *See also*, most recently, Nandini S Boodia-Canoo, *Slavery, Indenture and the Law Assembling a Nation in Colonial Mauritius* (Routledge 2023); Burkhard Schnepel, *Small Island, Large Ocean. Mauritius and the Indian Ocean World* (Routledge 2023) 70–131.

House of Nassau, chief of state of the provinces of the Dutch Republic, and after the main vessel of the fleet which was called 'Mauritius'. From then on, the island was used by the Dutch as a stopover after long months at sea. Dutch colonisation started in 1638 with the establishment of a small garrison intended to oversee the exploitation of the island's vast ebony forests by slaves brought from Madagascar. Numerous commanders were appointed, but continuous hardships such as cyclones, droughts, pest infestations, lack of food and illnesses interrupted the colonisation efforts and, finally, forced the Dutch to abandon the island in 1710. Yet, the collapse of the Dutch colony did not lead to the complete disappearance of human settlements on the island. Contemporary historians tend to believe that a small colony of fugitive slaves and deserters was formed in the remotest parts of the island.

B. The French Colonial Period (1715–1810)

8. Abandoned by the Dutch East India Company, the island became a French colony when, in September 1715, Guillaume Dufresne d'Arsel landed and took possession of this port of call on the route to India. He named the island 'Isle de France'. The French government turned over the administration of Mauritius to the French East India Company. However, the French were not to settle on the island until 1721. During the eleven years between the departure of the Dutch and the arrival of the first settlers, Isle de France was a largely abandoned island where pirates occasionally stopped for refreshments.

9. In December 1721, the French started their occupation as the first group of sixteen settlers arrived in the Port Louis area, where they built the first houses. Soon, they were joined by other batches of settlers coming from France, along with slaves brought from Réunion. However, it was only from 1735 on, with the arrival of the French governor, Bertrand-François Mahé de La Bourdonnais, that the development of Isle de France as a stable and prosperous colony started effectively. La Bourdonnais introduced order and discipline among the settlers and the slaves, established Port Louis as a naval base and is said to have motivated all categories of colonists to work for profit, especially to produce food for the passing ships of the French East India Company. Under his governorship, numerous buildings were built, a number of which still stand today, and an aqueduct was built to convey water from a cascade to the town of Port Louis.

10. After La Bourdonnais' departure in 1747, four governors led Isle de France, a well-established French colony, through the turbulent times of the Seven Years' War, until the French East India Company went bankrupt and the French crown took over the island's administration in 1767. According to a royal decree, the government of Isle de France was reorganised: the authority was split between a governor who controlled the police and the military and an 'intendant' who was in charge of financial and economic matters. The company's monopoly of trade ended, and the royal government authorised the inhabitants of Isle de France to trade in the Indian Ocean region, which was a prerequisite for a new phase of political, economic and social development. The first intendant, Pierre Poivre, took measures to stabilise agricultural prices, preserve the stocks of game, deer and fish, and stop the destruction of the island's forests. He invited the colonists to bring agricultural practices to a higher standard, for example, by planting spices such as nutmegs, cloves and breadfruit trees. The port was developed, and an engineer, Tromelin, did major work to increase its capacity and modernise its equipment. During royal rule, from 1767 to 1793, the population of Isle de France grew from a total of 19,000 to almost 50,000.

11. The year 1789 marked the beginning of the French Revolution which overthrew the monarchy in France and established a revolutionary government. The news of the events in France reached the island in January 1790, creating vivid tensions among the colonists of Isle de France and inviting the slave population to revolt. The Colonial Assembly, which was set up in 1789 and composed of representatives of the White population, adopted all the regulations passed by the Legislative Assembly in Paris as long as the interests of the slave-owners were not threatened. However, in March 1796, the Colonial Assembly refused to apply a law of February 1794 in Isle de France, by which the French revolutionary government ordered the abolition of slavery in the French colonies. In April 1796, the Colonial Assembly took over the control of the colony's finances from the French intendant. From that moment on, Isle de France became virtually an independent country, rebutting all attempts from the French government to regain control over the island. The French government, which had been engaged in a war against Great Britain since 1793, was not able to restore order in the former 'model colony'.

12. By 1802, when the British and the French signed the Peace of Amiens, the finances and the economy of Isle de France had improved, as the Colonial Assembly had used customs duties to finance public expenses. However, after the accession of Napoléon Bonaparte to power in France, the power of the Colonial Assembly declined and it was dissolved by the new government. Napoléon sent to Isle de France one of his ablest military officers, General Charles Decaen, who was proclaimed governor in September 1803. Decaen introduced the new Code Napoléon, re-established the judicial system that prevailed before 1789, reorganised the police as well as the local administration and set up a new organisation for port administration.

13. During the Napoleonic Wars, the Indian Ocean became an important strategic region, as numerous fleets of British vessels with goods crossed the trade routes between India and Europe. In 1808, the French government sent a frigate squadron to the Indian Ocean to augment the forces available in the region and raid British shipping from the ports of Isle de France and Reunion (then known as Ile Bonaparte). The raids continued until 1810, when a strong British expedition was sent to capture Isle de France. A preliminary attack was foiled at Grand Port in August 1810 (known as the 'Battle of Grand Port', immortalised on the Arc de Triomphe in Paris), but the main attack launched in November of the same year was successful. After ninety-five years, the French rule came to an end with the signature of the Treaty of capitulation by General Decaen on 3 December 1810.

C. The British Rule (1810–1968)

14. The terms of capitulation were particularly honourable for the French army and the colonists. The French troops were not considered prisoners of war and the inhabitants could 'preserve their religion, laws and customs', which is unique to British colonial history. Moreover, freedom was granted to the colonists to quit the colony with their respective private property; troops and sailors were sent back with their families to France on French and British ships. Baron d'Unienville, a famous Mauritian historian, observed that visitors to Port Louis would have been surprised that the only change they would find in town was the red (and no longer blue) dress of military sentries. As many rich colonists thought that their economic interests would be best served by cooperation with the British, they immediately started to collaborate with them. Upon restoration of peace in 1814, British sovereignty was confirmed by the Treaty of Paris and the name Mauritius was reinstated.

15. The British administration, which began with governor Robert Townsend Farquhar (1810–1823), was followed by rapid social and economic changes. From the early 1830s on, sufficient knowledge of the English language was a condition for employment in administration, and since 15 July 1847 (a day after 14 July, the French national holiday), the use of English was compulsory before the courts, showing the gradual retreat of the French language. Even more important was the abolition of slavery by the emancipation order of 1 February 1835 under the pressure of the British abolitionist movement. The planters received a total compensation of GBP 2 million for the loss of their slaves, 'imported' from Africa and Madagascar during the French rule.

16. After the emancipation order became fully effective in 1839, the newly emancipated slaves massively left the plantations to become small agricultural producers, self-employed artisans and fishermen, settling all over the island, founding numerous villages[3] and creating the need for a new cheap source of adaptable labour. Indentured labour began with Chinese, Malay, African and Malagasy labourers, but it was India which supplied a total of 500,000 labourers to Mauritius. This 'melting pot' of people from India, China, Africa and Europe lived in different ways. Whereas the bourgeoisie tended to adopt a Europeanised way of life, with a Francophile majority and an Anglophile minority, the other populations opted for the English language and English culture as a reaction to the economic and political supremacy of the Franco-Mauritians.

17. As the Indian population became numerically dominant and the right to vote was extended, political power shifted from the Franco-Mauritians and their Creole allies to the Indo-Mauritians. This important development took place in a difficult economic context. The malaria epidemic of 1866–68 drove shipping away from Port Louis, which further declined after the opening of the Suez Canal in 1869. Except for a short period during World War I, when sugar prices were particularly high, the

3. This has been documented for the municipality of Vacoas-Phoenix. *See* Sydney Selvon, *La genèse d'une ville. Vacoas-Phoenix* (Municipalité de Vacoas-Phoenix 1984).

Mauritian economy experienced a steady decline. The Great Depression of the 1930s led to violent conflicts between the Indian community (mostly sugarcane labourers or their descendants) and the Franco-Mauritians. Following this, the Mauritius Labour Party (MLP) was founded in 1936 to safeguard the interest of the labourers. World War II did not improve the Mauritian economy, and in 1938, the local British government enacted significant reforms that unbanned labour unions, improved channels of arbitration between labourers and employers, and improved working conditions.[4]

18. Elections in August 1948 for the newly created Legislative Council marked Mauritius's first steps toward self-rule. It was the first time that women were allowed to vote and a significant number of Indo-Mauritians and Creoles were elected. However, it was not until 1958 that universal suffrage was introduced in Mauritius. At the same time, an independence campaign gained momentum in Mauritius, as the British agreed to permit additional self-government and the government in London signalled that it had no intention of blocking independence for many British colonies. In 1967, the pro-independence parties, grouped under the banner of the Independence party, won a majority in the Legislative Assembly election, paving the way for a definitive political emancipation of Mauritius. But it would be a mistake to believe that the march to independence took place in a peaceful and serene climate; between 1965 and 1968, ethnic riots broke out and could only be brought under control with assistance from British troops who had to flow in from Southeast Asia. Eventually, despite the tense atmosphere, British rule ended on 12 March 1968 with the Mauritius Independence Act.

D. *Independent Mauritius (Since 1968)*

19. In the first years of independence, the government of Mauritius attempted to diversify its economy beyond the production of sugar but made only limited progress. The combined effects of falling world sugar prices, political protest and social unrest, still present on the island, led the government under Sir Seewoosagur Ramgoolam (also known as 'SSR') to initiate a substantial programme of economic diversification. The main engine of economic growth in the 1970s was the development of export-oriented industries and the tourism industry; during the period of 1974 to 1979, salaries increased by 30%, creating an air of general prosperity. The benefits of improved productivity allowed the government to reinforce the welfare state by introducing a national pension scheme, abolishing school fees and increasing subsidies to basic food supplies, such as rice and flour.

20. In 1991, the legislature voted to transition to a republican form of government, and on 12 March 1992, Mauritius became a republic; the last Governor General of Mauritius, Sir Veerasamy Ringadoo, became the first President of Mauritius and functioned as a ceremonial figurehead. However, the social situation remained

4. Richard Croucher & John McIlroy, *Mauritius 1938: The Origins of a Milestone in Colonial Trade Union Legislation*, 54 Labor History 223–239 (2013).

tense, in spite of the good economic performance of the country in the 1970s and 1980s (the 'Mauritius miracle'). Poorer people in Mauritius – largely Creoles – did not feel that they could share in the fruits of economic development or were adequately represented in politics. This led to large and unexpected outbursts of rioting and social unrest in 1999 following the death in a police cell of the popular singer Kaya. The government had great difficulty in restoring order and peace after those first real domestic disturbances since independence. At the beginning of the twenty-first century, unemployment rose, in part because of the detrimental effects of international trade on textile and sugar manufacturing. The government responded by focusing the country's economic strategies on the development of more lucrative sectors, such as information technology and business and financial services.

III. Political System

21. The Constitution of Mauritius came into force on 12 March 1968 following the adoption by the British parliament of the Mauritius Independence Act. It establishes a parliamentary democracy based on a Westminster system of government.[5] Since the country became a republic in 1992, Article 1 of the Constitution proclaims that 'Mauritius shall be a sovereign democratic State'. The National Assembly, Mauritius's unicameral house of parliament, elects the President and the Prime Minister. Whereas the President has a mostly ceremonial role, the Prime Minister of Mauritius enjoys significant power as the chief executive. He is thus the head of government and it is on his or her advice that the President appoints the members of the government. The Council of Ministers, responsible for the direction and control of the government, consists of the Prime Minister, the leader of the majority party in the National Assembly, and the ministers, including one Deputy Prime Minister and/or one Vice Prime Minister.

22. The National Assembly is a unicameral legislature consisting of seventy members. Sixty-two are directly elected for five-year terms in twenty-one constituencies; eight additional members, known as 'best losers', are appointed by the Electoral Supervisory Commission to ensure that ethnic and religious minorities are equitably represented and to correct any imbalance in community representation.[6]

---

5. *See also* Doorgesh Ramsewak, *The Constitution: Its Legal Aspect and Political Philosophy* (Proag Printing, 2nd ed. 1997); Ashwanee Budoo and Nora Ho Tu Nam, *The Republic of Mauritius. Introductory Note*, in *Oxford Constitutions of the World* (OUP 2016) 1–17; Jacques Colom, Stephanie Rohlfing-Dijoux & Götz Schulze (eds), *The 50th Anniversary of Mauritius. Constitutional Development* (Nomos 2019).
6. According to Section 3(4) of the First Schedule of the Constitution, 'the population of Mauritius shall be regarded as including a Hindu community, a Muslim community and a Sino-Mauritian community; and every person who does not appear, from his way of life, to belong to one or other of those three communities shall be regarded as belonging to the General Population, which shall itself be regarded as a fourth community'. On this system, *see* Raj Mathur, *Parliamentary Representation of Minority Communities; The Mauritian Experience*, 44 Africa Today 61–82 (1997); Yonathan Fescha and Nora Ho Tu Nam, *Is It Time to Let Go? The Best Loser System in Mauritius*, 28 Afrika Focus 63–79 (2015); Régis Lanneau, *Building a Common Identity in a Multicultural Society*

The political party or political alliance which wins the majority of seats in the National Assembly forms the government and its leader usually becomes the Prime Minister. The Government is primarily responsible for the National Assembly and the Prime Minister stays in office as long as he or she retains the support of a majority of its members.

23. The political system of Mauritius is also characterised by an independent judiciary which is not controlled by the executive or legislative branch. Mauritius has a single-structured judicial system consisting of the Supreme Court and the Subordinate Courts.[7] The Supreme Court is composed of a Chief Justice, a Senior Puisne Judge and seventeen Puisne Judges. According to section 76(1) of the Constitution, it has both original jurisdiction and appellate jurisdiction over all other courts of Mauritius, that is, the Intermediate Court, the Industrial Court, ten District Courts and the Court of Rodrigues, the Bail and Remand Court, the Criminal and Mediation Court and the Commercial Court, which are all magistrates' courts. Even though it is the highest court in Mauritius, its final judgments are subject to appeal to the Judicial Committee of the Privy Council (UKPC).[8] Special mention has to be made of the Director of Public Prosecutions who is appointed by the Judicial and Legal Service Commission of Mauritius and who is vested with the power 'to institute and undertake criminal proceedings before any court of law (…) (and) to take over and continue any such criminal proceedings that may have been instituted by any other person or authority'.[9]

24. The Republic of Mauritius has a multi-party system which is dominated by three left-wing or centre-left political parties, that is the Labour Party, the Militant Socialist Movement (MSM) and the *Mouvement Militant Mauricien.* Since independence in 1968, all governments of Mauritius have been led by one of those parties or an alliance led by them. Beyond party lines, it is important to note that the premiership of Mauritius has been alternating between two Indo-Mauritian families, the Ramgoolams and the Jugnauths, except for a short period of 2003–2005, where Paul Bérenger, of Franco-Mauritian descent, was Prime Minister under an alliance with the Jugnauths. In January 2017, the then Prime Minister, 86-year-old Sir Aneerood Jugnauth, a key political figure in Mauritian politics for many decades, announced that he was stepping down as Prime Minister. Following the British tradition, the leader of the governing party MSM, Pravind Jugnauth, who is Sir Aneerood Jugnauth's son, was sworn in as the new Prime Minister.

Through Electoral Rules, the Case of Mauritius, in *The 50th Anniversary of Mauritius. Constitutional Development* (Jacques Colom, Stephanie Rohlfing-Dijoux & Götz Schulze eds, Nomos 2019) 451–467.

7. For more details, *see* Milan Meetarbhan, *Cadre constitutionnel*, in *Le droit de l'île Maurice* (LGDJ, 2022) 33–34; Michael Bogdan, *The Law of Mauritius and Seychelles* (Jurisrörlaget i Lund 1989) 21–22; Anthony Angelo, *Mauritius: The Basis of the Legal System*, 3 CILSA, 228, 233–237 (1970).
8. The number of appeals to the Judicial Committee is about three to five per year and it seems that, even twenty-five years after the proclamation of the Republic of Mauritius, there are no plans of abolishing this legal remedy.
9. On the role of the Director of Public Prosecutions, *see* Jamil Ddamulira Mujuzi, *Private Prosecutions in Mauritius: Clarifying Locus Standi and Making the Director of Public Prosecutions more Accountable*, 10 African Journal of Legal Studies 1–34 (2017).

IV. Economic and Social Values

25. Since independence in 1968, the Government of Mauritius has decided to diversify the country's economy beyond its former dependence on agriculture and particularly sugar production.[10] While sugarcane is still grown on about 90% of the arable land area and accounts for 25% of export earnings, today's economy of Mauritius is a mixed developing economy based on agriculture, exports, financial services and tourism. With a well-developed legal and commercial infrastructure and a tradition of entrepreneurship and representative government, Mauritius is today seen as one of the African countries with the best foreign investment climate. Since the 1990s, in response to an economic slowdown due to stagnating exports and labour-market rigidities, the Government has tried successfully to modernise the sugar and textile industries, which in the past were overly dependent on trade preferences, while promoting diversification into areas such as information and communications technology, financial and business services, seafood processing and exports. Although the economic system of Mauritius has moved further towards freedom of entrepreneurship over the last fifty years, the Government still controls imports of rice, flour, petroleum products and cement.

26. The process of economic transformation is also connected to the establishment of so-called export-processing zones (EPZ), following similar schemes set out in Southeast Asia.[11] The Mauritius Export Processing Zone Act of 1970 provided investors with a series of incentives, including free repatriation of capital and dividends, guarantees against nationalisation, fiscal incentives and duty-free importation of machinery, equipment, spare parts and industrial inputs. By the 1990s, the Mauritian EPZ, with investments mostly coming from China, Hong Kong and Taiwan, surpassed the sugar industry as the principal export-earning sector and employed more workers than the agricultural sector and the government combined, which were previously the two largest employers. Currently, there are approximately 15,000 foreign workers, mainly from Sri Lanka, India and China, who are vital to the functioning of the EPZ. Since the 2000s, however, the Mauritian EPZ have faced serious challenges. With the expiration in 2004 of the Multi-Fiber Agreement regulating global trade in textiles and garments, companies were forced to close down their manufacturing sites due to rising costs. Other firms shifted their production to lower-cost producing industries, such as Mozambique and Madagascar, due to labour shortages and the rising cost of labour in Mauritius.

---

10. *See also* Vanessa Tang, Timothy Shaw & Merle Holden (eds), *Development and Sustainable Growth of Mauritius* (Palgrave Macmillan 2020); Ramola Ramtohul & Thomas Hylland Eriksen (eds), *The Mauritian Paradox. Fifty Years of Development, Diversity and Democracy* (University of Mauritius Press 2018); Indranarain Ramlall, *Economics and Finance in Mauritius. A Modern Perspective* (Palgrave Macmillan 2017); World Bank, *Mauritius. Inclusiveness of Growth and Shared Prosperity* (World Bank Group 2015); Sam Lingayah, *Social Welfare in Mauritius: a Critical Analysis of Social Service Provisions* (SanKris 1996).
11. Vanessa Tang, *Zoning in on Mauritius Special Economic Zones: Structure, Evolution and Economic Impact*, in *Development and Sustainable Growth of Mauritius* (Vanessa Tang, Timothy Shaw & Merle Holden eds, Palgrave Macmillan 2020) 105–117.

27. Mauritius has a comprehensive social protection system consisting of contributory social insurance programmes and non-contributory social assistance schemes, overseen and administered by the Ministry of Social Integration, Social Security and National Solidarity. The government allocates about 5.5% of the GDP to social protection, which is one of the highest rates for low- and middle-income economies. In particular, Mauritius is known for its universal old-age pension. Mauritius invests nearly 3% of the GDP to ensure that everyone who reaches the age of 60 years receives a state-financed pension. Indeed, absolute poverty among elderly people is almost nonexistent, and with a coverage rate of almost 100%, the National Pension Scheme, implemented in 1976, is one of the most effective pension systems in the world. The social protection system of Mauritius is completed by a national healthcare system, which is financed by taxpayers and free of any user cost, as long as the primary medical needs are concerned. Additional needs are dealt with in the private sector on a fee basis, either through out-of-pocket payments or payments by private health insurers.

§2. Legal System

I. Primacy of the Constitution and Legislation

28. The legal system of Mauritius follows the logic of a constitutional democracy based on the primacy of the Constitution of 1968 (as amended). According to section 2, the 'Constitution is the supreme law of Mauritius, and if any other law is inconsistent with this Constitution, that other law shall, to the extent of the inconsistency, be void.' The supremacy of the Constitution ensures that all laws enacted by Parliament are in conformity with the constitutional provisions. To guarantee the conformity of the legislation, the Constitution provides that any person who feels aggrieved that a provision of the Constitution has been infringed can apply to the Supreme Court to obtain redress. There are numerous examples in which the Supreme Court invalidated legislation which infringed individual rights vested by the Constitution,[12] contravened the principle of separation of powers,[13] or added a property qualification for standing for election, unprovided for by the Constitution.[14] This means that the doctrine of parliamentary sovereignty and the rule of law, which are dominant characteristics of the Westminster system, have a much different meaning in Mauritius than, for example, in the United Kingdom, where judicial review of constitutionality is not permitted.[15]

12. *Police v. Fra* [1975 MR 157] (legislation inconsistent with the presumption of innocence guaranteed by s. 10 of the Constitution).
13. *Mahboob v. Government of Mauritius* [1982 MR 135].
14. *UDM v. Governor General* [1990 MR 118].
15. *See* on this aspect Milan JN Meetarbhan, *Constitutional Law of Mauritius. Constitution of Mauritius with Commentaries* (2017) 16–19, 277–281; Olivier Desaulnay, *L'accès à la justice constitutionnelle à Maurice dans la Constitution de l'indépendance (1968–2018)*, in *The 50th Anniversary of Mauritius. Constitutional Development* (Jacques Colom, Stephanie Rohlfing-Dijoux & Götz Schulze eds, Nomos 2019) 193–207.

29. The Constitution of 1968 is based on the separation of powers and, as many other constitutions in the world, adheres to the idea of checks and balances with a division between the legislative, executive and judiciary branches.[16] In a landmark case of 1982, the Supreme Court stated that 'Parliament under our Constitution has no more right to pronounce judgments than the Supreme Court has the right to pass laws' and that 'the power of Parliament to make laws for the peace, order and good government of the country did not entitle Parliament to pass legislation which usurps the judicial power of the judicature'.[17]

30. Section 45(1) of the Constitution attributes law-making power to the parliament; it may pass laws 'for the peace, order and good government of Mauritius'. As noted before,[18] Acts of Parliament, referred to as primary legislation, must be in conformity with the Constitution. Subsidiary legislation refers to regulations which are enacted by ministers, local councils or other public authorities to whom law-making power is delegated. This means, in particular, regulations made by a minister and proclamations by the President. All statutory instruments are published in the *Government Gazette* and compiled in the *Revised Laws of Mauritius*, edited by the Attorney General's Office and, since 2007, by LexisNexis. As in other commonwealth jurisdictions, a Law Reform Commission was set up as an independent statutory body in 2015 in order to make recommendations for the reform and development of the law of Mauritius.[19] As of June 2024, more than 170 review papers, issue papers or discussion papers of high quality have been issued by the Commission.

31. The interpretation of statutory instruments follows the rules set out by the Interpretation and General Clauses Act 1974, which adheres to the principles elaborated by English courts. However, given the French origin of some legal terms without any equivalent under common law,[20] section 10 of this act provides that 'where in an enactment a French term or expression is used, or an English term or expression is explained by reference to a French term or expression, the interpretation of the enactment shall be in accordance with that of the French term or expression'. Unlike under English law, marginal notes, which briefly indicate the content of

16. On this doctrine in the Mauritian context, *see* Varsha M Chadee, *Application of the Separation of Powers Mechanism in a Unicameral Framework: the Case of Mauritius*, in *The 50th Anniversary of Mauritius. Constitutional Development* (Jacques Colom, Stephanie Rohlfing-Dijoux & Götz Schulze eds, Nomos 2019) 69–80.
17. *Mahboob v. Government of Mauritius* [1982 MR 135]. The Judicial Committee of the Privy Council confirmed this standpoint in a case concerning Mauritius (*Gilbert Ahnee & Ors v. The Director of Public Prosecutions* [1988 UKPC 28]).
18. *See* para. 28 above.
19. On the role of this commission, *see* Rosario P Domingue, *Contribution of Law Reform Commission to the Strengthening of Constitutionalism in Mauritius*, in *The 50th Anniversary of Mauritius. Constitutional Development* (Jacques Colom, Stephanie Rohlfing-Dijoux & Götz Schulze eds, Nomos 2019) 37–51.
20. It is not rare that the lawmakers use French legal terms in enactments drafted in English, especially when they refer to provisions of the Civil Code, the Code de Commerce and the Code de Procédure Civile, all of them drafted in French, or of the Criminal Code, partially drafted in French and English. *See*, for example, s. 28A(7) Prevention of Terrorism Act ('In any proceeding under this section, the Judge in Chambers may require the attendance of the Ministère Public.').

every section, are regarded as part of the enactment.[21] Earlier than in other common law jurisdictions, the Supreme Court held that Mauritian courts should be allowed to refer to parliamentary debates (referred to as *travaux préparatoires*) as an aid to interpretation in cases of ambiguity.[22]

32. While statutory enactments are almost entirely drafted in the English language and follow the common law tradition of legislative drafting,[23] the backbone of the legal system of Mauritius consists of three codes of French origin, which applied at the time of the transfer of sovereignty from France to the United Kingdom. Despite numerous amendments of both common law and French extraction, the Code civil, the Code de Commerce and the Code de Procédure Civile still bear a strong resemblance to the original codifications, which were drafted in France under the reign of Napoléon Bonaparte. As for the Criminal Code, it was enacted in 1838 in both French and English and is largely based on the Napoleonic *Code pénal* of 1810. This French heritage justifies the qualification of Mauritius as a mixed jurisdiction, as is widely acknowledged by comparative law scholars.[24] When interpreting the codes of French origin and, more widely, an enactment arising from French law, the courts of Mauritius seek guidance in the French legal literature and case law, as has been confirmed by the Supreme Court on a number of occasions.[25] However, it must be noted that, from time to time, the Supreme Court decides to depart from the French law when it considers that a different solution would be more adequate, as was the case, for example, when interpreting Article 1384 Civil Code.[26]

II. Position of the Judiciary

33. In theory, the Civil Code of Mauritius does not leave any room for case law among legal sources in Mauritius. According to Article 5, 'judges are forbidden to pronounce by means of general and statutory disposition on the cases brought before them'. It follows from this that court decisions, even when pronounced by

21. [1953 MR 37]. *See also* Anthony Angelo, *Mauritius: The Basis of the Legal System*, 3 CILSA, 228, 239 (1970).
22. *Madelen Clothing Co Ltd v. Termination of Contracts of Service Board & Ors* [1981 MR 284].
23. For a comparative survey of legislative drafting, *see* L Neville Brown, *British and French Statutory Drafting: A Review Article*, 37 ICLQ 696 (1988); William Dale (ed.), *British and French Statutory Drafting* (Institute of Advanced Legal Studies 1987).
24. *See* among others Vernon Valentine Palmer (ed.), *Mixed Jurisdictions Worldwide* (CUP, 2nd ed. 2012) 629–630; Jacques Du Plessis, *Comparative Law and the Study of Mixed Legal Systems*, in *Oxford Handbook of Comparative Law* (Mathias Reimann & Reimann Zimmermann eds, OUP, 2nd ed. 2019) 475, 483; Tony Angelo, *Mauritius: 'Capitulation, Consolidation, Creation'*, in *A Study of Mixed Legal Systems: Endangered, Entrenched, or Blended* (Sue Farran, Esin Örücü, & Seán Patrick Donlan eds, Ashgate 2014) 117–137.
25. *See*, for example, *Lingel-Roy & Ors v. The State of Mauritius & Anor* [2017 SCJ 411] ('It is appropriate to recall the practice that when it comes to the interpretation of a law borrowed from French law we stand guided for its interpretation by French doctrine and case law.'). *See also L'Etendry v. The Queen* [1953 MR 15].
26. In *Mangroo v. Dahal* [1937 MR 43], the Supreme Court decided that this text was not a statutory basis for a general principle of liability for the action of things. *See* para. 152 below.

the highest court, cannot be binding precedents. In light of this provision, one might assume that judicial decisions cannot be a source of law in Mauritius and that there is no rule of precedent, as is the case in France. However, following the common law tradition, decided cases form a genuine source of law in Mauritius, as the Supreme Court confirmed explicitly.[27]

34. This paradoxical situation can be explained by the circumstances under which British rule was enacted in Mauritius. While the British colonial administration was obliged to maintain the 'laws' previously in force according to Article 8 of the 1810 Treaty of Capitulation, there was a strong willingness on the part of the authorities to anglicise the procedure before courts and to introduce the English court system in Mauritius. When an 1850 Ordinance replaced the former *Cour d'Appel* with a Supreme Court, the ordinance invested it 'with all the powers, authority, and jurisdiction that are possessed and exercised by Her Majesty's Court of Queen's Bench in England'.[28] It was therefore only logical that the Supreme Court adopted the same procedure as its English counterpart and adhered to the doctrine of precedent.[29] This means that within the hierarchy of Mauritian courts, a lower court is always bound by a decision of a higher court (Supreme Court and Judicial Committee) on the same issue.[30] The Supreme Court is not bound by its own previous decisions but regards them as highly persuasive, and the view has been expressed that if the court wishes to overrule its own decision, it should sit as a full court.[31]

35. As is the case in many common law jurisdictions, the importance of case law must, however, be put in perspective. In areas regulated by statute, judicial decisions contribute to the normative process, indicating which provisions are applicable to a given situation and how a statutory rule is to be interpreted. There are only a few areas in the law of Mauritius that are entirely governed by case law (of common law origin):[32] contempt of court, judicial review of decisions of public authorities[33] and

27. *See The Director of Public Prosecutions v. Mootoocarpen* [1988 MR 195] ('It is quite clear that if a treatise were to be written on Mauritian Law, the sources of our law would not be limited to statute but would have to include case-law.').
28. Ordinance No. 2 of 1850 altering the organisation of the several courts of justice within the colony of Mauritius.
29. Rosario P Domingue, *The Historical Development of the Mixed Legal System of Mauritius During the French and British Colonial Periods*, 4 University of Mauritius Research Journal 1, 7–8 (2002).
30. Except in areas where the common law of England or equitable rules have been made applicable by Parliament, Mauritian Courts are not bound by decisions of English Courts.
31. *Rozemont v. The King* [1951 MR 61] ('When the point was raised again in the present case and this Court was asked to overrule the decision of 1925, I felt strongly inclined to leave he case to my brother judges and I would have gladly done so were it not for the fact that, in my judgment, if this Court can overrule a decision of its own it should, for that purpose, sit at its full strength.').
32. Rosario P Domingue, *Legal Method & Mauritian Legal System* (University of Mauritius 2003, Unit 2) 10–11 and by the same author *Sources du droit*, in *Le droit de l'île Maurice* (LGDJ, 2022) 22.
33. For more details, *see* John W Bridge, *Judicial Review in Mauritius and the Continuing Influence of English Law*, 46 ICLQ 787–811 (1997); Law Reform Commission, *Discussion Paper: Judicial Review* (Law Reform Commission 2010).

the law of evidence.[34] Moreover, section 16 of the Courts Act provides that the Supreme Court shall also be a court of equity, vested to do acts for the due execution of equitable jurisdiction in cases where no legal remedy is provided. This has led the courts to issue injunctions, a typical equitable remedy, without any statutory basis.[35]

III. Distinction Between Public and Private Law

36. The same ambiguity concerns the distinction between public and private law. Given the French origin of the law of Mauritius, it would not be surprising if the public law/private law distinction were a specific feature of this legal system. As is well known by comparative lawyers, civil law jurisdictions are characterised by a prominent role of public law, which is considered one of the main pillars of the legal system, along with private law and criminal law.

37. In France, the origins of the distinction between public and private law, often described as a 'summa divisio', go back to the turbulent post-revolutionary period, when the National Constitutional Assembly adopted an Act, still in force today, according to which 'judicial functions are and shall always remain separated from administrative functions. Ordinary judges shall not interfere in any way whatsoever with administrative matters, nor hear a claim brought against a public authority on account of their official duties'.[36] A significant consequence of the separation of ordinary courts and executive power was the emergence of a distinctive body of regulation governing administrative action. The progressive implementation of an administrative court system led to the formation of what is known today as *droit administratif*.[37] By contrast, the distinction is less fundamental in common law jurisdictions, where public law and administrative law are not seen as distinct branches of the legal system.[38] Public authorities tend to be subject to the same rules as private individuals and it is not until recently that the idea of distinct administrative courts for judicial review has emerged in the legal debate.[39]

34. *See* s. 162 Courts Act: 'Except where it is otherwise provided by special laws now in force in Mauritius or hereafter to be enacted, the English law of evidence for the time being shall prevail and be applied in all Courts of Mauritius.'
35. Domingue, n. 32, at 11. *See also* paras 51 and 269–271 below.
36. Article 13 of the Act of 16–24 Aug. 1790.
37. On this evolution, *see* in English Eva Steiner, *French Law: A Comparative Approach* (OUP, 2nd ed. 2018), 173–174; George A. Bermann & Étienne Picard, *Administrative Law*, in *Introduction to French Law* (George A. Bermann & Étienne Picard eds, Wolters Kluwer 2008) 57, 59–60; Hugo Flavier & Charles Froger, *Administrative Justice in France. Between Singularity and Classicism*, 3 BRICS Law Journal 80 (2016); Lionel Neville Brown, John Bell & Jean-Michel Galabert, *French Administrative Law* (OUP, 5th ed. 1998) 44–55, 126–128.
38. For a more complete survey, *see* J Allison, *A Continental Distinction in the Common Law: A Historical and Comparative Perspective on English Public Law* (OUP 2000).
39. In England, an Administrative Court was created in 2007 as a part of the Queen Bench's Division of the High Court of Justice.

38. The situation in Mauritius tends to be more impregnated by the common law understanding than by its French legal inheritance. There are no specific administrative courts, and besides legislation governing public authorities or activities specific to the government (taxation, administrative police, urban planning, etc.), the law of Mauritius does not provide for a coherent set of rules that is equivalent to a French-style *droit administratif*. The law of judicial review is almost entirely based on the English law[40] and, as in other common law countries, the idea is firmly established that, in principle, public authorities should be subject to the same rules of common or statutory law and to the same jurisdiction of ordinary courts as any private citizen. To give an example, section 2(1) of the State Proceedings Act provides that 'the State shall be subject to all those liabilities in tort to which, if it were a private person of full age and capacity'.

39. However, in specific areas, the influence of French law tends to surface. As will be seen, in the field of tort law, the Supreme Court holds that, despite the assimilation of the State to a private person according to section 2(1) of the State Proceedings Act, a claimant has to establish a 'gross fault' or *faute lourde*, a prerequisite directly inspired by the French administrative law.[41] Furthermore, it is remarkable that, by contrast to the British tradition, the concept of State is widely used in Mauritius as a corporation aggregate vested with a legal personality, co-existing with different parts or components of government (a particular Minister or official), acting as representatives of political power.[42]

IV. Sources of Private Law in General and of Tort Law in Particular

40. The private law of Mauritius is mostly the product of Napoleonic codification, the Civil Code of Mauritius being its primary source. By virtue of an 1805 decree,[43] the Civil Code of 1804 was put into effect for the French colonies in the Indian Ocean, and in 1808, a decree signed by General Decaen extended to Mauritius the re-promulgation and renaming of the Code.[44] From then on and for almost two centuries, the Civil Code was known as the *Code Napoléon*. It was only in 1981

40. Bridge, *supra* n. 33; Rajendra P Gunputh, *Le modèle du contentieux administratif anglais dans la Constitution et la fonction publique des anciennes colonies françaises dotées d'un système de droit mixtes. Le cas de l'île Maurice*, 15 University of Mauritius Research Journal 405–426 (2009).

41. *State of Mauritius v. Sookna* [2001 SCJ 51]. For more details, *see* para. 100 below.

42. The situation in England is more complex as it differs in administrative law and in contract. For a complete survey, *see* Janet McLean, *The Crown in Contract and Administrative Law*, 24 OJLS 129–154 (2004).

43. Decree of 17 Oct. 1805, known as Act 109/1805. *See* Éric Agostini, *Actualité des codes français à l'île Maurice*, in *Apprendre à douter: questions de droit, questions sur le droit – Études offertes à Claude Lombois* (Pulim 2004) 37, 38.

44. Decree of 21 Apr. 1808, better known as the French Civil Code Re-Promulgation Act 1808. *See* Louis Venchard, *Codes annotés de l'île Maurice*, vol. 1 *Code Civil* (Law Publishers, 1st ed 1983) v.

that the Parliament of Mauritius adopted the name of *Code civil de Maurice*,[45] and it is not rare that recent legislative acts still refer to the Civil Code as the *Code Napoléon*.[46]

41. Although revised in several fields of law (such as personal status, family law or rights of creditors), the Civil Code of Mauritius still bears a strong resemblance to the original codification of French descent. For Mauritian lawyers, it serves as a fundamental working tool, and law students in Mauritius are trained, from the first year of their studies, to become familiar with its structure and provisions. The Civil Code is divided into three 'books' (*livres*) dedicated to the legal status of persons (Book I), things and the modifications of ownership (Book II), and the 'various ways how ownership is acquired' (Book III).[47] Surprisingly, the main source of the law of obligations is Book III of the Civil Code of Mauritius, the title of which may evoke to foreign lawyers the law of property or real estate rather than a body of rules governing contracts and torts. This Book is also the most voluminous, covering various subjects grouped into twenty sections (*chapitres*). While it is understandable that the *Code civil* drafters conceived contracts as a means to acquire ownership of things (section 3 is dedicated to 'contracts and conventional obligations in general'), it is way more difficult to see in the rules on civil liability some kind of regulation on the acquisition of ownership. Yet, this presentation, inherited from Roman law, has not been altered over the decades.

42. As for the tort law of France, one of the most singular features of the Mauritian tort law is the concise nature of its legislative framework. Since the Civil Code entered into force in 1805 in Mauritius, the rules governing extra-contractual civil liability are laid out in only five provisions (Articles 1382–1386), which have remained unchanged since then, apart from some additions to Article 1384 concerning the general principle of liability for things and the specific cases in which the spreading of fire (*propagation d'incendie*) is the origin of harm.[48] Unlike in France, the Mauritian authorities did not deem it useful to implement specific rules on product liability or liability for road traffic accidents, so the common rules of civil liability are of much more significance than under French law.[49]

43. To give the reader an overview of the (few) provisions on civil liability, what follows is an English translation of Articles 1147 (on contractual liability) and 1382 to 1386 (on extra-contractual liability):[50]

---

45. Section 7(1) of the Revision of Laws (Amendment) Act 1981 ('There shall be published as a separate volume in a revised edition a Code which shall be known as the Code Civil Mauricien.').
46. *See* for example s. 50(1) Copyright Act ('Article 910 of the Code Napoleon shall not apply to the Society.').
47. On the structure of the French Civil Code, *see* Jean-Sébastien Borghetti, *French Law*, in *The Scope and Structure of Civil Code* (Julio César Rivero ed., Springer 2013) 181–200.
48. Section 48 of the Code Napoleon (Amendment No. 3) Act 1983.
49. *See* paras 171–182 below.
50. Two semi-official English translations of the French Civil Code are available: a 2014 version prepared by a team of academics from law schools in Louisiana (David Gruning, Alain A Levasseur & J Randall Trahan) and a 2006 version prepared by Georges Rouhette and Anne Rouhette-Berton. The

Article 1147

A debtor shall be ordered to pay damages, if there is occasion, either by reason of the non-performance of the obligation, or by reason of delay in performing, whenever he does not prove that the non-performance comes from an external cause which may not be ascribed to him, although there is no bad faith on his part.

Article 1382

Any act, whatever of man, which causes damage to another, obliges the one by whose fault it occurred, to compensate it.

Article 1383

Everyone is liable for the damage he causes not only by his intentional act, but also by his negligent conduct or by his imprudence.

Article 1384

(1) A person is liable not only for the damages he causes by his own act, but also for that which is caused by the acts of persons for whom he is responsible, or by things which are in his custody.
(2) The father and mother, in so far as they exercise parental authority, are jointly and severally liable for the damage caused by their minor children who live with them.
(3) Masters and employers, for the damage caused by their servants and employees in the functions for which they have been employed;
(4) Teachers and craftsmen, for the damage caused by their pupils and apprentices during the time when they are under their supervision.
(5) The guardian (*gardien*) of a thing, for the damage caused by the action of it.
(6) The above liability exists, unless the father and mother or the craftsmen prove that they could not prevent the act which gives rise to that liability or unless the guardian of the thing proves that the damage was caused by force majeure or the victim's exclusive fault.
(7) However, a person who possesses, regardless of the basis thereof, all or part of a building or of movable property in which a fire has originated is not liable towards third parties for damages caused by that fire unless it is proved that the fire must be attributed to his fault of to the fault of persons for whom he is responsible. This provision may not apply to the landlord and tenant relationship, which remains governed by Articles 1733 and 1734 Civil Code.

---

following excerpt has been taken from the latter. *See also* the translation by Olivier Moréteau, *France*, in *European Tort Law. Basic Texts* (Ernst Karner, Ken Oliphant & Barbara Steininger eds, Jan Sramek Verlag, 2nd ed. 2018) 123–140.

Article 1385

The owner of an animal, or the person using it, during the period of usage, is liable for the damage the animal has caused, whether the animal was under his custody, or whether it had strayed or escaped.

Article 1386

The owner of a building is liable for the damage caused by its collapse, where it happens as a result of lack of maintenance or of a defect in its construction.

44. While the substance of the Civil Code in France and Mauritius is still identical, the numbering of the articles of the French Civil Code has departed from the original version of the Code Napoléon and the Civil Code currently in force in Mauritius, especially since the reform of the French law of obligations in 2016.[51] As Mauritian courts and legal scholars often refer to the French texts, it may be useful to give the reader a correlation table:

Civil Code of Mauritius	*French Civil Code Before 1 October 2016*	*French Civil Code since 1 October 2016*	*Liability Regime*
Article 1382 Article 1383	Article 1382 Article 1383	Article 1240 Article 1241	Fault-based liability
Article 1384(2)	Article 1384(4)	Article 1242(4)	Parental liability
Article 1384(3)	Article 1384(5)	Article 1242(5)	Liability of employers for the acts of employees
Article 1384(4)	Article 1384 (6) and (8)	Article 1242 (6) and (8)	Liability of teachers for the acts of pupils
Article 1384(5)	Article 1384(1)	Article 1242(1)	General principle of strict liability for things
Article 1384(6)	Article 1384(7)	Article 1242(7)	Exemption clause for parental liability (and for the strict liability for things)
Article 1384(7)	Article 1384(2) and (3)	Article 1242(2) and (3)	Fault-based liability for harm caused by the spreading of fire
Article 1385	Article 1385	Article 1243	Liability for damage caused by animals

51. Even though there has not been any modification to tort law provisions, the 2016 reform did introduce a significant formal change, as Articles 1382 to 1386 (extra-contractual liability) and 1147 (contractual liability) were renumbered to take into account the new structure of section 3 of Book III.

Civil Code of Mauritius	*French Civil Code Before 1 October 2016*	*French Civil Code since 1 October 2016*	*Liability Regime*
Article 1386	Article 1386	Article 1244	Liability for damage caused by collapsing buildings
N.A.	Article 1386-1–1386-18	Article 1245–1245-17	Product liability
Article 1147	Article 1147	Article 1231-1	Contractual liability

45. Given the lawmakers' inertia in the field of civil liability, both in Mauritius and in France, it is not surprising that the courts have developed a comprehensive body of judge-made tort law rules. More so than in other fields of law, a foreign lawyer is far from understanding the civil liability rules only by consulting the relevant provisions in the Civil Code. The mere existence of a codification does not necessarily mean that the legislation has an answer for any legal problem, especially in a jurisdiction where the Civil Code only contains five articles dedicated to tort law.[52] What characterises the Mauritian tort law system is that, on several occasions, the Supreme Court had to interpret the provisions of the Civil Code in order to adapt the tort law rules to a changing society, often (but not always) drawing directly on the case law developments in France. The most topical example is the liability for things (*responsabilité du fait des choses*), which was 'discovered' by the French Court of Cassation in the late nineteenth century when confronted with new social risks arising from industrialisation.[53] At an initial stage, the Supreme Court of Mauritius decided to depart from the French interpretation of Article 1384(1) Civil Code, favouring a fault-based approach for the liability for things. It was only in 1983 that the Parliament added a new paragraph to Article 1384, enshrining the principle of strict liability for things in the Civil Code.[54]

46. When interpreting the Civil Code provisions, the judges of Mauritius do not hesitate to refer to the legal writings of French scholars. As early as 1861, the Supreme Court admitted that 'where questions are raised on the Civil Code, we are in the habit of resorting to the (…) writings of the eminent lawyers of the country which gave it birth'.[55] It is natural for legal professionals to consult French textbooks and treatises, in particular as scholarly efforts made by legal professionals and the few law academics have not yet given rise to a comprehensive body of legal

52. Hein Kötz, *Taking Civil Codes Less Seriously*, 50 Modern Law Review 1 (1987). *See also* René David, *The Civil Code in France To-Day*, 34 Louisiana Law Review 907, 911 (1974).
53. *See* paras 152–166 below.
54. Venchard, *supra* n. 44, at 398. *See also* Rajendra P Gunputh, *Traité de droit civil mauricien* (Star Publications, 2nd ed. 2019) 848–855.
55. *Carbonel, Bourdin Fils & Co v. Letellier & Ors* [1861 MR 51].

doctrine.[56] What may strike a foreign observer are the repeated references in Supreme Court judgments to classical authors of the French legal doctrine rather than to contemporary sources. To quote an author, 'numerous writers are regarded as "*autorités*" for the Civil Code: Aubry & Rau, Baudry-Lacantinerie, Planiol & Ripert, Colin & Capitant, Troplong, Marty & Raynaud, Mazeaud, etc.'[57] However, the availability of French databases providing access to an up-to-date legal documentation has rejuvenated the legal references to French legal scholarship in more recent times.

47. In May 2017, the Law Reform Commission of Mauritius issued a discussion paper on a future reform of the tort law provisions of the Civil Code.[58] In this paper, the Commission emphasises the need for a reform in an area where the legislation dates back to 1804, carrying out a comparative study of the French reform projects[59] and the statutory and case law developments in Mauritius.[60] Despite the Commission's thorough analysis, a tort law reform has been considered neither by the Government nor by the lawmakers of the National Assembly.[61]

§3. Function of the Law of Torts

48. As in many other jurisdictions, the primary function of the tort law of Mauritius is the compensation of harm caused by the tortfeasor. According to a notable formula adopted by the French Court of Cassation and regularly cited by the Supreme Court of Mauritius, 'the proper function of civil liability is to re-establish as exactly as possible the balance disturbed by the harm and to replace the victim in the situation in which he would have been if the harm had not occurred'.[62] Thus, the main objective of civil liability is the restoration of the *status quo ante*. From this derives the principle of full reparation, known in the law of Mauritius as the '*principe de réparation intégrale du préjudice sans perte ni profit*',[63] which is one of the fundamental concepts of the French law-based tort law, admitting only a few exceptions. As will be seen below,[64] the remedies awarded to the victim shall be equivalent to the harm suffered and encompass all consequences of the harm, may

56. On the need for a genuine Mauritian legal doctrine, *see* Rajsomer Lallah, *Report of the Committee on the Review of Legal Studies in Mauritius* (Supreme Court 1983).
57. Domingue, *supra* n. 32, at 15.
58. Law Reform Commission, *Discussion Paper: Reform of Law on Responsabilité Civile in the Code Civil Mauricien* (Law Reform Commission 2017).
59. On these projects, *see* Jonas Knetsch, *Tort Law of France* (Wolters Kluwer 2021) para. 43, n. 45.
60. Law Reform Commission, *supra* n. 58, at 5–160.
61. It is worth noting that the Civil Code of Seychelles, dating back to the French Civil Code of 1804 and translated from French to English in 1976, has undergone a substantial review from 2011 to 2020, under the guidance of the then Chief Executive Officer of the Law Reform Commission of Mauritius. *See* on this reform Anthony H Angelo & Sarah Mead, *A New Civil Code in Seychelles*, 26 Comparative Law Journal of the Pacific 299–310 (2021).
62. *See* for example *Berque Ltd v. Pigeot & Anor* [2021 SCJ 157]; *South Gate Island Tours v. Tarsoo* [2021 SCJ 341] The formula is borrowed from René Savatier, *Traité de la responsabilité civile en droit français* vol. 2 (LGDJ 2nd ed 1951) para. 601.
63. *See* for example *Cooppen & Anor v. New India Assurance Co Ltd* [2019 SCJ 152].
64. *See* paras 227–250 below.

they be of pecuniary or non-pecuniary nature. Even though there is a common understanding of the incommensurability of distress or other non-pecuniary losses, the principle of full compensation is considered the legal basis of damages for pain and suffering and loss of enjoyment of life.

49. Unlike in France, the expansion of liability insurance and the development of a comprehensive social protection system have not led to a paradigm shift in the field of tort law. When comparing the rules on civil liability in France and Mauritius, a discrepancy is immediately noticeable between the victim-oriented compensation rules adopted by the French courts and the Mauritian approach based on the primacy of liability for fault and on the principle that a loss should lie where it falls, unless it may be shifted to another person for specific reasons. It is doubtful that tort lawyers from Mauritius would support the idea that the rules on civil liability should primarily serve the interests of claimants and that a 'lack of coverage', especially in cases of personal injury, necessarily calls for a legislative reform or a revision of the case law. The emergence of a 'compensation of ideology', well documented in France,[65] seems to be a long way off in Mauritius.

50. There are many reasons that could explain this rather traditional approach to tort law. First, liability insurance coverage is not as widespread as in other countries with similar economic strength.[66] With the notable exception of motor vehicle insurance (third-party insurance is compulsory under section 55 of the Road Traffic Act 1962), the 'insurance culture' is not well developed among professionals and private individuals, which means that, in many tort law cases, there is no insurance company with deep pockets behind the tortfeasor, a tort law claim being a serious financial threat for the defendant. Second, it is very likely that the common law-based tort law culture has influenced the tort law of Mauritius more than is generally believed. Even though contemporary studies reveal that the reality of litigation is much different, the fault principle still plays a major role in the English law, whereas strict liability, especially when it derives from statute, is a largely neglected field of torts.[67]

51. As to other secondary functions of tort law, such as deterrence (*fonction préventive*) and sanction (*fonction punitive*), there does not seem to be a scholarly debate about the appropriateness of introducing punitive damages in the law of Mauritius. According to the current state of legislation, there is no room for damages with a punitive character, that is, exemplary damages. In particular, Article 1382 Civil Code does not allow claimants to ask for anything other than compensatory damages. This was confirmed by the Supreme Court in divorce litigation

65. *See* Knetsch, *supra* n. 59, at para. 45 (with further references).
66. Insurers' Association of Mauritius, *Insurance Report 2020* (2021) 12 ('general insurance penetration by individuals and MSMEs (excluding motor as this is mandatory) is quite low.'). *See also* Dimitri Vassas, *The Insurance Industry in Mauritius* (World Bank 2003) 9–13.
67. *See* Richard Lewis & Annette Morris, *Tort Law Culture in the United Kingdom: Image and Reality in Personal Injury Compensation*, 3 JETL 230, at 240–241 (2012).

cases.[68] However, in the field of defamation, there seems to be a tendency for claimants to ask for the award of exemplary damages, especially since the courts decide to consistently award damages in the amount of MUR 300,000.[69] While the Supreme Court does not assert the punitive character of those damages, one could argue that the fixed-price nature of the amount and the absence of correlation from the claimant's situation indicate a practice of disguised punitive damages.

52. Should tort law also address situations in which an individual is facing a risk of imminent harm? Whereas, under French law, there is an ongoing debate on the link between civil liability and prohibitive injunctions (*actions en cessation de l'illicite*),[70] this issue appears to have been raised neither in case law nor in legal scholarship. Under English law, injunctions operate as an important tool, by which the court can order the defendant to stop a continuing or recurring act, especially in cases in which the loss to be inflicted would be of such a character that the claimant could not practically be compensated in damages. It is rather common for the courts of Mauritius to grant injunctive reliefs to claimants, in particular during the pre-trial (or interlocutory) stage.[71] However, the case law does not make it clear on which legal basis the courts award prohibitive injunctions. As section 16 of the Courts Act provides that the Supreme Court shall also be a court of equity, one can assume that this remedy preserves its equitable origins from the English law despite the civil law-based tort context.[72]

§4. Relationship Between Torts and Criminal Law

53. When it comes to the relationship between tort and crime, the law of Mauritius follows the traditional English law approach, according to which criminal courts should not be involved in awarding compensation, regarded as a classic (and

68. *Tandrayen (h) v. Tandrayen (w) and Babajee* [1973 SCJ 40]; *Gardette (h) v. Gardette (w) and Nageon de Lestang* [1954 MR 107]. In a previous case, the Supreme Court decided that in assessing damages courts should be guided by English authorities (*Ramduth v. Ramduth and Ah Soy* [1946 MR 1]).
69. *Mohamed Sayar & Ors v. Austin* [2019 SCJ 61]. According to this judgment, 'perusal of the most recent awards in defamation cases reveals that the Courts have consistently awarded damages in the sum of MUR 300,000 (vide *Neewoor v. Burrenchobay* [2017 SCJ 22], *Dayal v. Advance Publications (Mauritius) Co Ltd* [2017 SCJ 94], *Jyoti's Clinic Ltd v. Le Mauricien Ltd* [2018 SCJ 113] and *Cinemax Ltd v. Le Mauricien Ltd* [2018 SCJ 139])'.
70. Knetsch, *supra* n. 59, at para. 48. *See also* in the English language Paula Giliker, *Injunctions Requiring the Cessation of Unlawful Action*, in *French Civil Liability in Comparative Perspective* (Jean-Sébastien Borghetti & Simon Whittaker eds, Hart 2019) 377.
71. For an illustration in the field of nuisance, *see* the case *Canarapen L v. J Anne* [1999 SCJ 293]. For more details, *see* paras 269–271 below.
72. In its 2017 discussion paper on the reform of civil liability rules, the Law Reform Commission simply states that 'there is no mention of the preventive function of civil liability in our Civil Code, whereas it should be considered to implement it'. *See* Law Reform Commission, *Discussion Paper on the Reform of Law on Responsabilité Civile in the Code Civil Mauricien* (2017) para. 11.

exclusive) domain of the law of torts.[73] According to section 7(1) of the Criminal Procedure Act, '(n)o prosecution at the suit of the State shall be joined with a civil action, but a private party in whose behalf a prosecution has been instituted may bring an action for damages in a civil Court against the offender'. This means that, unlike under French law, victims of criminal offences cannot bring an *action civile* before criminal courts to seek for compensation of their harm;[74] their lawyer will deal with criminal and civil liability as two separate issues and will claim damages before a civil court and not a criminal judge. In contrast to the situation in the United Kingdom, the lawmakers in Mauritius did not adopt a legislative act to involve criminal courts in awarding compensation.[75]

54. What is more, section 7(2) of the Criminal Procedure Act provides that '(t)he verdict or judgment in the one case shall not be admitted as evidence in the other', which is even more surprising for a tort lawyer with a continental European background.[76] To understand this specific feature of common law, it should be kept in mind that civil and criminal procedure rules differ fundamentally from each other, with one of the major differences being the standard of proof. While facts have to be proven on the balance of probabilities for tortious claims, criminal courts will apply the more severe standard of 'beyond reasonable doubt'.[77] This also explains why, in Mauritius (as well as in England), neither criminal convictions nor acquittals bind a later civil court on substantive questions of law. In this context, the Supreme Court held in *Jamodhee v. Jharia* that '(e)ven if in civil proceedings arising from the same facts evidence of a conviction is sometimes allowed to show that there has been a prosecution and a conviction, the result of the criminal proceedings is not admissible as evidence in the civil proceedings'. It is therefore not uncommon that an acquitted defendant is found liable in tort at the subsequent civil litigation.

§5. Relationship Between Contractual and Extra-contractual Liability

55. Another major topic of debate is the relationship between contractual and extra-contractual liability. The Civil Code of Mauritius does not contain any explicit rule on this issue, and the Supreme Court is still struggling to provide clear and

73. For a recent presentation, *see* Matthew Dyson & John Randall, *England's Splendid Isolation*, in *Comparing Tort and Crime: Learning from Across and Within Legal Systems* (Matthew Dyson ed., CUP 2015) 18; Matthew Dyson, *Explaining Tort and Crime* (CUP 2022) 220–296.

74. On the French *action civile*, *see* in the English language Knetsch, *supra* n. 59, at paras 49–53.

75. On the UK Powers of Criminal Courts (Sentencing) Act 2000, *see* Dyson & Randall, *supra* n. 73, at 54–55.

76. *Jamodhee v. Jharia* [2013 SCJ 148]. *See also* more recently *District Council of Savanne v. Luchmun & Ors* [2021 SCJ 127].

77. Under French law, a criminal offence recognised as such by the criminal courts also constitutes a fault (*faute*) for the purpose of fault-based liability under Articles 1240 and 1241 Civil Code. On this principle, known as the theory of the 'unity of criminal and civil faults' (*identité des fautes civiles et pénales*), *see* Knetsch, *supra* n. 59, at para. 52.

accurate solutions, as is the French Court of Cassation, by the way. One of the distinctive features of the tort law of Mauritius is the rule known as *non-cumul*; its implications are manifold, even though the rule is not as far-reaching as under French tort law. Given the practical importance of choosing the appropriate cause of action, it is essential to start by presenting the specific features of contractual liability before delving into the meaning of the *non-cumul* rule and the scope of contractual liability.

I. The Distinctiveness of Contractual Liability

56. In Mauritius, like in other jurisdictions, the consequences of non-performance of contractual obligations are a constant subject of debate. While there is consensus on the relevance of the concept of *responsabilité contractuelle* (a French expression regularly used in the Supreme Court case law),[78] the differences between contractual and extra-contractual liability are a far more critical issue to review as they determine the orientations regarding the interplay between both liability regimes.

57. The first discrepancy between contractual and extra-contractual liability is about the standard of liability, as the non-performance of a contractual obligation does not necessarily correspond to a fault under Articles 1382–1383 Civil Code. A contract can indeed give rise to an *obligation de résultat,* the breach of which is characterised by the mere fact that the promised outcome has not been reached;[79] thus, the proof of non-performance is not always based on an assessment of the defendant's conduct. Second, the concepts of liability for acts of others or for the acts of things cannot be easily transposed to *responsabilité contractuelle* as it is usually irrelevant whether the non-performance can be attributed to the act of another person or to the defect of a thing: the contractual partner is accountable for both.[80] Third, there are major differences when it comes to the consequences of liability and the regime applicable to compensation claims. Even though the modalities of compensation are similar (damages or *réparation en nature*), Article 1150 Civil Code provides that 'a debtor is liable only for damages which were foreseen or which could have been foreseen at the time of the contract'. As a consequence, the assessment of contractual damages implies not only taking into account exemption or

78. *See* recently *VSDJ Properties Ltd v. Ramanand Boodhun* [2023 SCJ 286].

79. For an application of this idea in a traffic accident liability case, *see Beniot & Anor v. UBS & anor* [2022 INT 107] ('it is clear that [United Bus Service] had a contractual obligation to carry plaintiff No. 1 safe and sound to his destination from the time he boarded the said bus as a paying passenger').

80. Regarding the situation under French law, *see* in particular Geneviève Viney, *Introduction à la responsabilité* (LGDJ, 4th ed. 2019) paras 258–266 and, in English, Geneviève Viney, *Tort Liability*, in *Introduction to French Law* (George A Bermann & Étienne Picard eds, Wolters Kluwer 2008) 241–242. *See also* Emmanuelle Juen, *La remise en cause de la distinction entre la responsabilité contractuelle et la responsabilité délictuelle* (LGDJ 2016) 421–520.

limitation clauses but also, more generally, the expectations of the contracting parties.[81] Finally, when it comes to the regime governing compensation claims, actions under contract are subject to different limitation periods,[82] jurisdiction and conflict-of-law rules.

II. The Meaning of the Non-cumul Rule

58. Although widely known by comparative tort law scholars, the rule of *non-cumul* is not what its name suggests. There has never been any suggestion that the coexistence of contractual and extra-contractual liability could allow a claimant to 'cumulate' damages both on a contractual and a tortious basis.[83] What is meant by the term *non-cumul* is that a contracting party is not entitled to damages from the other party in tort as long as the loss has been caused by the non-performance of a contractual obligation. Therefore, the expression *non-cumul* actually reflects a 'no-choice rule'[84] which indicates that in cases of overlap of contract and tort,[85] contract law prevails. Surprisingly, there is absolutely no legal basis for this rule in the Civil Code; it was elaborated by the French civil courts in the early twentieth century in order to preserve the rules governing contractual liability from the wide general liability clause based on *faute* and the absence of restrictions regarding the compensation of pure economic loss under extra-contractual liability.[86]

59. In Mauritius, while the *non-cumul* rule is deeply entrenched in the tort law system and constantly reaffirmed by the Supreme Court, case law is still abundant in the interplay between contractual and extra-contractual liability, even nowadays. Over the last decade, there has not been a single year without at least three or four

81. *See* in the English language Solène Rowan, *Remedies for Breach of Contract: A Comparative Analysis of the Protection of Performance* (OUP 2012) 114–117.
82. A legislative reform in 1978 has reduced the general limitation period for 'personal claims' (*actions personnelles*), regardless of the contractual or extra-contractual background, to ten years (Article 2270 Civil Code). However, there are still specific limitation periods for contractual claims between merchants and for specific types of contracts (Articles 2273–2281 Civil Code; Articles 103, 296, 371 Commercial Code). For more details, *see* Law Reform Commission, *Issue Paper: Law of Prescription under Code Civil Mauricien* (2013).
83. *See* in particular *TFP International Ltd v. Itoola* [2002 SCJ 147] according to which 'the problem is one of "option" and not "cumul" since according to certain authors and a number of decided cases a breach of contract would give an aggrieved party an option between an action in tort or in contract at his choice depending on which of the two is deemed to be the more favourable'.
84. Almost every tort law scholar insists on the mismatch between the term *non-cumul* and the actual meaning of this rule and encourages the use of alternative expressions such as *non-option*. Unfortunately, old habits die hard, especially among lawyers and 9,000 kilometres away from France.
85. Which is very likely given the broad sense of fault under Articles 1382–1383 Civil Code. *See* paras 68–79 below.
86. *See,* e.g., Jean-Sébastien Borghetti & Simon Whittaker, *Introduction*, in *French Civil Liability in Comparative Perspective* (Jean-Sébastien Borghetti & Simon Whittaker eds, Hart 2019) 1, 5. For a more detailed presentation, *see* Viney, *Introduction*, *supra* n. 80 at paras 360–379. For a comparative study, *see* Tony Weir, *Complex Liabilities*, in *International Encyclopedia of Comparative Law* vol. XI (André Tunc ed., Brill & J C B Mohr 1983) paras 47–72.

judgments on the issue of *non-cumul*. In most cases, it is a question of rectifying the legal basis of a claim for damages with plaintiffs invoking an extra-contractual *faute* instead of the non-performance of a contract.[87] As a consequence, there is no doubt that the *non-cumul* rule applies in Mauritius and that a compensation claim under tort will not succeed if the harm was caused by the non-performance of a contractual obligation.[88]

60. Yet, the primacy of contract is not an absolute one and Mauritian case law allows for exceptions to the *non-cumul* rule. Until recently, the Supreme Court admitted that in case of gross negligence (*faute lourde*), an action for damages could be brought on the basis of extra-contractual fault under Article 1382 Civil Code.[89] The reason was that if the breach of contract amounts to a *faute lourde*, that should allow the claimant to benefit from certain advantages of an action in tort, especially to avoid the application of a disclaimer of liability or other limitation clauses. In other words, 'a plaintiff who wishes to plead *faute lourde* rather than breach of contract should be allowed to proceed in accordance with that option (…) having regard to our rules and tradition in relation to pleadings and to the spirit of fairness and justice'.[90] In a 2017 landmark case, the Judicial Committee reminded the Mauritian courts, however, that 'the gravity of the breach does not alter the fact that it is founded on the non-performance of an obligation which arose from the contract'.[91] The Committee held that the pre-existing case law was not satisfactory, criticising that the Supreme Court 'did not clearly differentiate between *faute lourde* as a factor disentitling the guilty party from relying on a limitation clause as a matter of contract law and the more radical concept of it giving rise to an independent cause of action not under contract law'.[92] Ever since, the Supreme Court of Mauritius has adopted a more classical stance on the application of the *non-cumul* rule, deciding that 'tortious liability can exist only where contractual liability does not; the rule is not concurrence but incompatibility'.[93]

61. While *faute lourde* is no longer an exception to the *non-cumul* rule, since *Mediterranean Shipping Company v. Sotramon*, it is uncertain whether another exception is valid under Mauritian law. Under French law, the most important

87. *See*, e.g., *N. R. Naik & Ors v. Widow C. Rampersad & Ors* [2023 SCJ 16].
88. *See* already *Kinoo v. Currumthaullee and Anor* [1977 MR 363]. *See also Data Communications Ltd v. The State of Mauritius & Anor* [2017 SCJ 319], *Coindreau v. Lemasson* [2017 SCJ 354], *Jaulim Plaza Ltd v. Bramer Banking Corporation Ltd & Anor* [2017 SCJ 368] et *Ampro Ltd v. Mauritius Eagle Insurance Co Ltd* [2017 SCJ 389].
89. *L'Inattendu Co Ltd v. Cargo Express Co Ltd* [2001 SCJ 7]; *La Patinoire Ltée v. Lakepoint Ltd* [2013 SCJ 344].
90. *Sotramon Limited v. Mediterranean Shipping Company* [2015 SCJ 109]. *See also Cascadelle Distribution et Cie Ltée v. Nestlé Products (Mauritius) Ltd* [2015 SCJ 120].
91. *Mediterranean Shipping Company v. Sotramon Limited* [2017 UKPC 23]. On this case, *see* Jonas Knetsch, *Le principe de 'non-cumul' entre les responsabilités délictuelle et contractuelle en droit mauricien*, The New Bar Chronicle 2018, No. 6, 24; Jean-Baptiste Seube, *Responsabilité contractuelle et délictuelle à l'Île Maurice*, IJLS Law Journal 2019, No. 9.
92. *Mediterranean Shipping Company v. Sotramon Limited* [2017 UKPC 23].
93. *See*, e.g., *Côte Ouest Audiovisuel Maurice v. Dearham M. A.* [2019 SCJ 343].

exception to the *non-cumul* principle is related to cases of a breach of contract punishable under criminal law, for example, constituting the offences of involuntary homicide (*homicide involontaire*) or involuntary personal injuries (*violences involontaires*).[94] According to the French Court of Cassation, the compensation claim brought before a criminal court is subject to the rules governing extra-contractual liability, even though the same claim brought before a civil court would be judged in contract. Strongly criticised by several authors,[95] this case law is based on the idea that only a 'delictual fault' (*faute délictuelle*) can be the basis of an *action civile* presented to a criminal court.[96] Due to the strict separation between criminal and civil liability and the absence of *action civile* under the law of Mauritius,[97] it is highly unlikely that the Supreme Court will admit the same solution as the Court of Cassation. However, the solution has not been ruled out either for now and the idea of a gravity threshold for a cause of action independent of contract is still very vivid among Mauritian lawyers.[98]

62. In addition to that, there are cases in which a defendant can only claim damages in tort despite a context more or less related to a contractual relationship. Indeed, pre-contractual liability is, in principle, subject to fault-based liability (Articles 1382–1383 Civil Code), for example, in cases of an excessively late withdrawal from negotiations or a lack of fairness during negotiations.[99] The same applies to post-contractual liability, for instance, in cases of the violation of a non-compete obligation after the termination of an employment contract.[100] Finally, in two older cases, the Supreme Court held that public notaries (*notaires*) are liable on an extra-contractual basis because of their monopolistic competences,[101] even though in more recent cases, it tends to admit a choice between an action in tort and an action in contract.[102]

---

94. *See* Yves-Marie Laithier, *The Relationship between Contractual and Extra-Contractual Liability as between Parties to a Contract*, in *French Civil Liability in Comparative Perspective* (Jean-Sébastien Borghetti & Simon Whittaker eds, Hart 2019) 37, 49.
95. For example, Viney, *Introduction*, *supra* n. 80 at para. 368; Michèle Muller, *L'inexécution pénalement répréhensible du contrat* (thesis Paris 2, 1976) paras 161–217.
96. From a comparative standpoint, *see* Christian von Bar & Ulrich Drobnig, *The Interaction of Contract Law and Tort and Property Law in Europe. A Comparative Study* (Sellier 2004) paras 294–304.
97. *See* paras 52–53 above.
98. *See*, e.g., *SUV Construction Ltd v. Sarah Jane Sam Fat* [2023 INT 32].
99. For an extensive study of the situation under French law, *see* Paula Giliker, *Pre-Contractual Liability in English and French Law* (Kluwer 2001) 105. *See also* by the same author *A Role for Tort in Pre-Contractual Negotiations?*, 52 ICLQ 969, 979–985 (2003); *Regulating Contracting Behaviour: The Duty to Disclose in English and French Law*, 13 ERPL 621 (2005). For a case under Mauritian law, *see La Brasserie Investment Ltd v. Wagnemeyer & Anor* [2022 INT 357].
100. *See* the interlocutory judgment in *Kirsh Co Ltd v. Reesaul & Anor* [2022 SCJ 406].
101. *Procureur Général v. Jollivet* [1892 MR 19]; *de Sornay v. de La Roche* [1924 MR 80]; *Péril v. de Robillard* [1916 MR 40].
102. *De Guardia de Ponte v. Parklane Properties & Ors* [2021 SCJ 16]; *Tirbooman & Anor v. Ramkissoon & Anor* [2023 SCJ 48].

III. The Scope of Contractual Liability

63. In light of the distinctiveness of contractual liability and given the *non-cumul* rule, it is important to set out the precise scope of contractual liability. To put it simply, a liability claim between two contracting parties is subject to the law of contracts if a breach of the contract (*inexécution contractuelle*) has caused a loss to one of them. This implies not only the existence of a valid contract between the claimant and the defendant but also a loss which can be attributed to the non-performance of a contractual obligation. These two requirements may seem obvious, but especially the second one has given rise to many uncertainties, as French law has taken a very broad approach to the perimeter of contractual obligations. At the beginning of the twentieth century, the Court of Cassation introduced with respect to contracts of carriage an implied 'safety obligation' (*obligation de sécurité*), which allowed passengers who suffered personal injury during the transportation to sue the carrier for damages on the basis of contractual liability. Since then, the *obligation de sécurité* has been extended to various other contracts in which the health or safety of one of the parties is at risk.[103] Mauritian courts have implemented this doctrine into the civil liability system, especially in cases of traffic accident cases in which the claimant had concluded a contract of carriage with a transportation company.[104] It is, therefore, not uncommon for Mauritian lawyers to deal with personal injury cases that do not fall within the scope of extra-contractual liability but lie solely within the area of contracts.

64. In the same spirit, the law of Mauritius provides that in the context of 'contractual groups', a client can sue for damages in contract even though the defendant is not the other contracting party, provided that the individual contracts are 'homogeneous'. This solution is based on a well-established case law in France, according to which the right to compensation on a contractual basis is attached to the defective material as an accessory (*accessoire*) running automatically with the goods to whoever becomes their owner.[105] In 1991, the Court of Cassation limited this solution to cases in which all contracts in the chain imply a transfer of ownership (*chaînes translatives de propriété*).[106] In a landmark decision in 2022,[107] the Supreme Court decided to transpose this solution into the law of Mauritius. In a case in which the claimants, who purchased a defective electric fan that caused a fire, claimed compensation both from the vendor and the distributor, the Court held that

103. *See,* e.g., Steiner, n. 37, at 85 (illustration of the complex interplay between case law and legislation); Pierre Catala & Tony Weir, *Delict and Torts: A Study in Parallel Part I*, 37 Tulane Law Review 573, 576 (1963). From a comparative standpoint, *see* Hein Kötz, *European Contract Law* (OUP, 2nd ed. 2017) 106–108 ('collateral duties').

104. For an example, *see Beniot & Anor v. UBS & anor* [2022 INT 107].

105. Ass plén, 7 Feb. 1986, No. 83-14631 (for an English translation *see* https://law.utexas.edu/transnational/foreign-law-translations/french/case.php?id=1294). On this case law, *see* the more detailed analysis in the English language by Kötz, *supra* n. 103, at 329–331.

106. For a critical assessment of this solution, *see* Jean-Sébastien Borghetti, *Breach of Contract and Liability to Third Parties in French Law: How to Break the Deadlock?*, ZEuP 2010, 279, 284. *See also* Simon Whittaker, *Privity of Contract and the Law of Tort: the French Experience*, 15 Oxford Journal of Legal Studies 327, 354–357 (1995).

107. *Donald & Anor v. King Bros Co Ltd & Anor* [2022 SCJ 143].

'the plaintiffs may have against (…) the sole distributor of Pacific fans in Mauritius, is a contractual one and the failure to ground their action in contract is wrong'.[108] Explicitly invoking the French case law, the court explained that 'the present plaintiffs are debarred from bringing an action in "tort" because in effect the obligation to provide a product free of any defect that can cause damage and prejudice is, as submitted, a contractual obligation which the manufacturer has with the ultimate buyer of that product'.[109]

65. Closely related to the extension of the contractual duties and the personal scope of contractual liability is the case law on the liability of contracting parties towards third parties, which reveals another source of complexity. According to *Vestalane Investments v. Federal Trust*, if the non-performance of a contractual obligation causes a loss to a third party, the claimant has to establish all the elements required to establish liability for *faute* under Article 1382 Civil Code, that is a fault, a reparable loss and a causal link.[110] However, the Supreme Court added, somewhat ambiguously, that 'in order to establish its case, the plaintiff must prove "une exécution défectueuse du contrat" and secondly that such "exécution défectueuse" has caused prejudice to it' and that 'such prejudice must be personal to the plaintiff, and must be distinct from any prejudice sustained by the party who is a victim of the breach under the contract'.[111] The ambiguity concerns the fact that establishing *faute* under Article 1382 is not the same as invoking the non-performance of a contractual obligation, which is not necessarily correlated to the violation of a general duty. It is therefore not yet clear whether a breach of contract could as such be a source of liability for the contracting party vis-à-vis a third party, like under French law, or whether the claimant has to establish the non-compliance with the general duty to act diligently.[112]

§6. Protected Interests

66. As under French law, the tort law of Mauritius is eager to provide full compensation for all varieties of loss, providing, of course, that all other requirements for civil liability are fulfilled. The system of liability, built on Articles 1382 to 1386 Civil Code, does not contain any definition of what should actually be understood

108. *Donald & Anor v. King Bros Co Ltd & Anor* [2022 SCJ 143].
109. *Donald & Anor v. King Bros Co Ltd & Anor* [2022 SCJ 143].
110. *Vestalane Investments (Pty) Ltd v. Federal Trust (Mauritius) Ltd* [2013 SCJ 217]. The solution was reiterated in *NY-Link Logistics Ltd v. Maersk (Mauritius) Ltd* [2019 SCJ 151].
111. *Vestalane Investments (Pty) Ltd v. Federal Trust (Mauritius) Ltd* [2013 SCJ 217].
112. The leading case is Ass plén, 6 Oct. 2006, No. 05-13255, commented in Olivier Moréteau, *France*, in *ETL 2006 (2007)*, 196, paras 32–41. *See also* Philippe Stoffel-Munck, *Liability of Contracting Parties Towards Third Parties*, in *French civil liability in comparative perspective* (J-S Borghetti & S Whittaker eds, Hart 2019) 55; Jean-Sébastien Borghetti, *Breach of Contract and Liability to Third Parties in French Law: How to Break the Deadlock?*, ZEuP 2010, 279, 287–292.

by 'reparable loss' (*préjudice réparable*), making it particularly 'claimant-friendly';[113] no distinction is made between interests relevant under tort law and those which are not protected.

67. It is only in very limited cases that the Supreme Court decided to bar a compensation claim on the grounds that the affected interest of the claimant is not protected under law. In particular, this issue arose when the Mauritian courts were confronted with compensation claims of unmarried partners (concubines). In the case of *Moutou*, the Supreme Court held that a concubine could not invoke an *intérêt juridiquement protégé*, explaining that the claim is to be based upon a 'lien of juridical nature'; otherwise 'the hairdresser, the tailor and all the purveyors of Plaintiff's late paramour, might sue the Railway Department for the loss they have sustained by the untimely death of their customer'.[114] This position has been followed until today,[115] and in a 2019 case, the Supreme Court decided that, unlike for religious marriages, the legislature of Mauritius did not intervene to give an official status to unregistered partnerships or *concubinage*.[116] As a consequence, the Court considered that 'given the limited intervention of the legislator on this particular issue (…), it will not be appropriate for us to adopt the liberal attitude as proned by the French Courts'.[117]

113. For an assessment of the French law of torts, *see* Jean-Sébastien Borghetti, *The Culture of Tort Law in France*, 3 JETL 158 (2012).
114. *Moutou v. Mauritius Government Railways* [1933 MR 102].
115. *Naikoo v. Société Héritiers Bogun* [1972 MR 66]; *Jugessur & Ors v. Bestel & Anor* [2007 MR 151].
116. *Lingel-Roy Mrs M J E M v. The State Of Mauritius & Anor* [2019 SCJ 103].
117. *Lingel-Roy Mrs M J E M v. The State Of Mauritius & Anor* [2019 SCJ 103]. On the situation under French law and the *Dangereux* case of 1970, *see* Steiner, n. 37, at 266; Knetsch, *supra* n. 59, at para. 283.

Part I. Liability for One's Own Acts

Chapter 1. General Principles

§1. Concept of Fault

68. In Mauritius, a civil fault is not necessarily a violation of a precise provision of Mauritian legislation. Of course, an individual driving faster than permitted by the law[118] will commit not only a criminal offence of 'speeding'[119] but also a civil fault that may give rise to civil liability *vis-à-vis* the victims of that tort. The above-mentioned civil fault results from the violation of section 124 of the Road Traffic Act of 1963.[120] Moreover, a person who kills intentionally another one will not only commit a crime, punished by section 216[121] of the Criminal Code,[122] but also a civil fault entailing his or her tort liability towards the members of the victim's family. Fault can be defined as the violation of a general duty not to harm another person unjustly.[123] This broad definition is perfectly in line with Articles 1382[124] and 1383[125] Civil Code, which does not define the notion of civil fault; both provisions only mention two types of it, namely intentional fault, on the one hand, and negligence and imprudence, on the other hand. Anyway, civil fault in Mauritius has to be defined as an error in the behaviour of an individual.

118. According to this text '(n)o person shall drive a motor vehicle of any class or description on a road at a speed exceeding that which may be prescribed as the maximum speed in relation to a vehicle of that class or description'.
119. This provision states that '(a)ny person who drives a motor vehicle on a road at a speed exceeding a prescribed speed limit (…) shall commit an offence'.
120. Act No. 22/1962.
121. This text states that '(m)anslaughter committed with premeditation or by lying in wait is murder'.
122. Act No. 6/1838.
123. This definition arises from French civil law, which is a persuasive authority in Mauritius. *See* for example Rémy Cabrillac, *Droit des obligations* (Dalloz, 14th ed. 2020) para. 241.
124. According to this provision, '(any act, whatever of man, which causes damage to another, obliges the one by whose fault it occurred, to compensate it'.
125. This provision states that '(e)veryone is liable for the damage he causes not only by his intentional act, but also by his negligent conduct or by his imprudence'.

§2. DUTY OF CARE

69. In Mauritius, there is no specific provision in the Civil Code on the elements of which the civil fault is composed. Traditionally, there are two elements on which the notion of civil fault is based:

(1) the ability of the tortfeasor to discern;
(2) the inadequate behaviour of the tortfeasor.

70. The ability to discern represents the intellectual capacity of an individual to understand the consequences of his acts[126] and to differentiate between wrong and right. This element of the civil fault gives a moral dimension to it: if an individual is able to understand the consequences of his or her act, then he or she will be able to regret it. An individual may be liable in tort only if he or she is morally liable and if he or she has the opportunity to regret the consequences of his or her act.

71. However, the concept of civil fault has considerably changed under French law between 1968 and 1984. As French civil law is a persuasive authority in Mauritius, it has to be briefly set out here. The first important change in France was made by a 1968 Act which provides for the tort liability of grown-up individuals, 18 years old or more, even if they have not had the capacity to discern in the moment when committing a civil wrong. In other words, even insane individuals may commit a civil fault and may be declared liable in tort. It is obvious that this change has had a strong impact on the notion of civil fault: an individual may be declared liable in tort even though he or she does not have the capacity to discern. The new rule is based on the requirements of justice and equity: to give compensation to the victims of harm even though the tortfeasor is unable to grasp the consequences of his acts.[127]

72. However, the 1968 Act did not apply to minors under the age of 18, whereas many of them, especially those who are of the age of 13 or less, do not have the capacity to differentiate between wrong and right. This is why the French Cour de cassation, which is an important persuasive authority in Mauritius, handed two important judgments on 9 May 1984[128] in which it stated that even minors, 3 or 11 years old, may commit a civil fault if their behaviour is not what may be expected in given circumstances from a reasonable and careful person. It means that, henceforth, civil fault is evaluated in an objective way: the tortfeasor's inability to discern is not taken into consideration; all that matters is that the defendant's behaviour was not in line with what has been expected from a reasonable and careful person in the same circumstances.

---

126. Knetsch, *supra* n. 59, at para. 80.
127. Knetsch, *supra* n. 59, at para. 81.
128. Cass Ass Plén, 9 May 1984, D 1984, jur 525.

73. In Mauritius, this objective approach was adopted in *Medine Sugar Estate v. Anthony.*[129] In the case of 1990, a very young child climbed over a 74 cm high protection wall and entered a tiger's cage. It was obvious that such a young child did not have the capacity to discern, i.e., he was unable to grasp the consequences of his acts. In spite of that, the Supreme Court attached to his behaviour the consequences of a civil fault.

74. Thus, the main question in Mauritius pertaining to the notion of civil fault is to ascertain the test applied by a judge or a magistrate while assessing the existence or the absence of a civil fault of the tortfeasor. There are two tests that could possibly be used in order to evaluate whether a tortfeasor's behaviour was in line with what has been expected from a reasonable and careful person in the same circumstances.

75. The first test is called *évaluation in concreto* of the civil fault. This test is inclusive of specific and personal circumstances of tortfeasors, such as their level of intelligence being lower than an average level, their physical defects, and the behaviour adopted in everyday life. This test is too favourable to tortfeasors as it allows them to avoid tort liability by proving that they had exactly the same behaviour as the one they have in their everyday lives or that the harm is due to the above-mentioned personal circumstances. In those cases, no civil fault can be linked to the defendants, in spite of the fact that they acted in a way in which an average and careful individual would not have acted had he or she been placed in identical circumstances.

76. As the test set out above seems to be unfair to the victims and too lenient for the tortfeasor, in Mauritius, civil fault is evaluated *in abstracto.*[130] The behaviour of a tortfeasor is compared to what an average and careful individual would have done in identical circumstances. Reference is made to an abstract model of an 'average and careful individual', which is usually a higher standard than the defendant's standard of care used in the *in concreto* test. The *in abstracto* test has been applied in the cases *Neron Publications Co Ltd v. La Sentinelle Ltd & Ors* of 2020,[131] *Hurnam v. Dabee* of 2010,[132] *Belloguet & Anor v. Mungur & Ors* of 2019,[133] *Cundasawmy v. The Government of Mauritius* of 2001[134] and *Ungnoo & Anor v. State of Mauritius* of 2005.[135]

77. It has to be noted that one personal circumstance of the defendant is taken into consideration in the *in abstracto* test, and that is his or her occupation. A judge or a magistrate will need to ascertain whether the tortfeasor has done everything that

129. 1990 SCJ 334.
130. *See*, under French law, Stéphanie Porchy-Simon, *Droit des obligations 2022* (Dalloz, 14th ed. 2021) para. 798.
131. 2020 SCJ 63.
132. 2010 INT 244.
133. 2019 SCJ 218.
134. 2001 SCJ 69; 2001 MR 25.
135. 2005 SCJ 89.

a careful person having the same professional qualification and the same experience would have done in identical circumstances. If the answer is a positive one, the defendant has not committed a civil fault and will not be liable in tort.However, if the answer to the above question is no, the defendant will be liable. For instance, an inappropriate medicine prescription and the duration of the medical care shorter than it should have lasted will qualify as the doctor's civil fault.[136] Moreover, the lack of proper monitoring of a child's broken arm that leads to gangrene and the amputation thereof is also a doctor's civil fault.[137]

78. Those general rules on the evaluation of the existence of a civil fault in Mauritius are confirmed in some specific laws of common law origin in Mauritius. Thus, according to section 37(1) of the Trusts Act of 2011, '(a) trustee shall in the exercise of his functions, observe the utmost good faith and act (a) with due diligence; (b) with care and prudence; and (c) to the best of his ability and skill'. That means that, under the law of Mauritius, the civil liability of trustees will depend on whether their behaviour has been in line with what an average and prudent trustee having the same professional qualifications and experience would have done in the same circumstances or not. If the trustee did not act in line with what an abstract reference model would have done in the same circumstances, his or her tort liability may be applied.

§3. Capacity

79. In Mauritius, as already explained, an individual may be declared liable in tort even though he or she does not have the capacity to discern. In other words, the capacity to discern does not form part of the notion of civil fault. Thus, infants and minors may commit a civil fault and be liable in tort. The main case law on this issue is the case *Medine Sugar Estate v. Anthony* of 1990.[138] In that case, a very young child climbed over a 74 cm high protection wall and entered a tiger's cage. It was obvious that such a young child did not have the capacity to discern, i.e., he was unable to grasp the consequences of his acts. In spite of that, the Supreme Court attached to his behaviour the consequences of a civil fault. Considering that the lack of compensation would be socially unjust in those cases and given the availability of liability insurance coverage for children and disabled adults, the French legislator introduced in 1968 a new provision in the Civil Code stating that 'a person who has caused damage to another when he was under the influence of a mental disorder is nonetheless liable to compensation'.[139] The Court of Cassation had already ruled a few years earlier that a person whose misconduct occurs during a state of dementia was nevertheless liable for the damage caused by a vehicle under his custody.[140]

136. *Belloguet & Anor v. Mungur & Ors* [2019 SCJ 218].
137. *Cundasawmy v. The Government of Mauritius* [2001 SCJ 69].
138. 1990 SCJ 334.
139. Article 414-3 Civil Code.
140. Civ 2, 18 Dec. 1964, D 1965, jur 191.

Chapter 2. Specific Cases of Liability for Fault

§1. Liability of Professionals

I. In General

80. In Mauritius, there is no higher standard of care for professionals compared to other individuals. Civil fault is evaluated *in abstracto*, i.e., the behaviour of a defendant is compared to what could be reasonably expected from a careful and reasonable person in the same circumstances, based on the professional qualifications and experience of the tortfeasor. In other words, the existence of a civil fault of the defendant depends on whether he or she has done everything that can be reasonably expected in the same circumstances from a reasonable and careful individual who has the same professional qualifications and the same professional experience. If yes, he or she has not committed any civil fault and will not be liable in tort. If not, he or she will be liable in tort for the harm suffered by the victim of his fault.

II. Medical Practitioners

81. In Mauritius, the medical profession is governed by the Medical Council Act 1999, the Nursing Council Act 2003 and the Code of Practice. The Medical Council Act sets out the requirements that have to be met to allow for the practice as a doctor in Mauritius. Section 21 of the Act stipulates that every person interested in being registered as a medical practitioner in Mauritius, living in Mauritius or abroad, shall personally apply to the Registrar. The application must be accompanied by the original or a certified copy of the applicant's medical degree. In the case of a specialist, the application must be accompanied by the original or a certified copy of the applicant's specialist qualification. When the medical degree or specialist qualification is written in a language other than English or French, a certified translation thereof in English or French must be provided. The evidence of any pre-registration training completed by the applicant must be presented with the application. The applicant's birth certificate or other acceptable evidence of his or her identity and any other document that the Medical Council might require form the applicant must be submitted together with the application.

82. When an applicant fulfils all the criteria set out by the Law, he or she will be registered as a medical practitioner in Mauritius. Section 22 of the Act determines who may be registered as a general practitioner in Mauritius. An applicant who wishes to be registered as a general practitioner in Mauritius must be a citizen of the Republic of Mauritius; must be a holder of prescribed degrees, including medical degree; must have undergone not less than eighteen months of practical (including clinical) training in medicine; must have successfully undergone an examination for the purpose of determining whether he possesses adequate professional medical knowledge; must be of good character and must not be convicted of an offence in any country involving fraud or dishonesty; must be mentally and physically fit, etc.

According to section 23 of the Act, any registered general practitioner in Mauritius may be registered as a specialist if he or she has the necessary specialist qualification.

83. The Nursing Council Act sets out the requirements that have to be met in order to become a registered nurse in Mauritius. Section 21 of the Act stipulates that every person who wishes to be registered in Mauritius as a nurse has to submit his application accompanied by the original or the certified copy of his qualifications; a certified translation in English or French of the qualification when the qualification is in a language other than English or French; the applicant's birth certificate or any official documentary evidence and any other document that the Council might require. Sections 22 and subsequent of the Act specify the requirements that have to be fulfilled for several various types of nurses, such as general nurse, specialised nurse, mental health nurse, midwife and state-enrolled nurse or assistant nurse.

84. It has to be noted that the Medical Council Act and the Nursing Act do not address the issue of civil fault or the issue of tort liability of doctors and nurses.

85. The Code of practice, issued by the Medical Council, sets out, first of all, the general duties of medical practitioners (Part I: Preamble), such as the duty to devote themselves to the service of suffering humanity in the field of medicine; to practise his or her profession with conscience, dignity and integrity; to maintain the utmost respect for human life at all times from the moment of conception till death; to offer his or her knowledge, skill and time to any person in need of medical attention without any distinction or discrimination and to uphold and maintain the dignity and honour of the medical profession (Item 1). Second, the Code (Part II) provides for a certain number of specific duties of a medical practitioner such as the duty to respect the patient's right to visit the registered medical practitioner of his choice (Item 1), the duty to obtain the informed consent of his patient in any case of medical intervention or medical research (Item 2), the duty to provide a lifesaving treatment in emergency, even if it is impossible to gain the patient's (next of kin's) consent (Item 4), the duty to treat a patient in case of an emergency (Item 5), the duty to inform his or her patient or the next of keen correctly about the true nature of the patient's illness (Item 7), the duty to find a qualified replacement (Items 8 and 10), the duty not to expose his or her patient whether by investigation or treatment to unnecessary risks (Item 11), the duty not to prescribe or supply drugs of addiction or dependence otherwise than in the course of bona fide treatment (Item 12), the duty not to disclose without authorisation any information imparted to him by a patient in relation to his treatment (Item 13), the duty not to exercise medical profession if the medical practitioner is in a state of intoxication due to alcohol or drug abuse (Item 14), etc.

86. In spite of a long list of professional duties of a medical practitioner in Mauritius, aiming at preservation of the integrity and quality of the medical profession, the Code of practice does not define the notion of civil fault of a medical practitioner. It is sure that a behaviour contrary to a duty set out in the Code of practice constitutes a civil fault and may entail the tort or contractual liability of a medical practitioner. However, there is no *numerus clausus* of civil faults under the law of Mauritius and the civil fault of a medical practitioner may also exist in case of a breach of a professional duty not listed in the Code of practice.

87. Indeed, the civil liability of medical practitioners, whether employed in public hospitals, in private clinics or as private practitioners,[141] will be assessed according to the general rules of tort liability, i.e., Articles 1382–1383 Civil Code.

88. The behaviour of a medical practitioner will be compared to what an average and careful medical practitioner having the same qualifications and experience would have done in identical circumstances. If he or she has done everything that an average and careful medical practitioner having the same qualifications and experience would have done in identical circumstances, there is no civil fault or tort liability. However, if he or she has not done everything that an average and careful medical practitioner having the same qualifications and experience would have done in identical circumstances, he or she will be liable in tort. For instance, an inappropriate medicine prescription and the duration of the medical care shorter than it should be will qualify as a doctor's civil fault.[142] Moreover, the lack of proper monitoring of a child's broken arm that leads to gangrene and the amputation thereof is also a doctor's civil fault that entails his tort liability.[143]

89. It has to be noted that in Mauritius, when, because of an emergency, a generalist had to intervene instead of a specialist, the doctor's civil fault will be assessed according to what might be reasonably expected from a generalist in the same circumstances and not according to what might be expected from a specialist.[144] It would be unfair and unjust to impose on a tortfeasor the duty to behave in line with what is expected from a person having superior qualifications and experience.

III. Legal Practitioners (Barristers and Attorneys)

90. Section 2 of the Law Practitioners Act 1984 defines a law practitioner as 'a barrister, an attorney or a notary whose name has been entered on, and not been erased from the Roll'. The Act does not specifically address the issue of the tort liability of law practitioners, but it sets out a certain number of duties, the breach of which will certainly lead, in some cases, to the civil liability of a law practitioner. Thus, section 3 of the Act stipulates that no person in Mauritius will provide legal services if he is not properly registered and is not a member of the Mauritius Bar Association, the Mauritius Law Society or the *Chambre des notaires*. Section 13 of

141. Goran Georgijevic, *La responsabilité civile des médecins employés par des hôpitaux publics à Maurice* (2021) Revue de droit international et de droit comparé 522–545, para. 3.
142. *Belloguet & Anor v. Mungur & Ors* [2019 SCJ 218].
143. *Cundasawmy v. The Government of Mauritius* [2001 SCJ 69].
144. *Ungnoo & Anor v. State of Mauritius* [2005 SCJ 89].

the Act provides for the disciplinary proceedings for an act done by a law practitioner, such as failing to comply with or to take such measures as are required under the Financial Intelligence and Anti-Money Laundering Act or the United Nations (Financial Prohibitions, Arms Embargo and Travel Ban) Sanctions Act 2019, or any regulations made or guidelines issued under those Acts. There is no doubt that a serious act leading to disciplinary liability may also constitute a civil fault and lead to the tort liability of a law practitioner. However, the Act does not give any additional detail on the nature of the acts that qualify as professional and civil fault. Section 15A imposes upon barristers and attorneys the obligation to issue a receipt to their clients for every sum received (e.g., deposit, fees, reimbursement of travelling expenses) in performing their legal services. In order to avoid unfair practices, section 17 of the Act stipulates that no person in Mauritius shall induce or seek to induce a client of a law practitioner to cease to be the client of that law practitioner or not to become a client and become the client of any other law practitioner. Section 18 of the Act adds that a law practitioner who draws up or prepares a document in the exercise of his profession shall sign and date the document.

91. It needs to be highlighted that a breach of some of the rules set out above will lead to the tort liability of a law practitioner, as the faults committed by him or her are related, to a certain extent, to the contract made with his or her client, but do not reveal any inexecution or bad execution of the contract,[145] whereas there are also the faults that will entail the contractual liability of the law practitioner, as they constitute an inexecution or a bad execution of the contract made with the client. Thus, in case where the liability of a barrister or attorney would be an extra-contractual one, the common rules on the tort liability set out in Articles 1382–1383 Civil Code are applicable to law practitioners. The test applied to assess the existence or the absence of a civil fault of a barrister or attorney is the same as for any other tortfeasor in Mauritius: the tort liability of a barrister or attorney will be applied if he or she commits an act that is contrary to what may be expected in the same circumstances from a reasonable and careful barrister or attorney who has the same qualifications and the same experience as the defendant.

IV. Builders and Architects

92. There are a few specific rules in the Mauritian Civil Code addressing the issue of the liability of builders and architects. Thus, according to Article 1792 Civil Code, if a building is totally or partially destructed due to a defect in the construction or to a defect in the land on which the building has been put up, the architects and the builders are liable for those defects for ten years. This constitutes a guarantee for the client who is protected against the civil faults that an architect or a

145. For instance, the exercise of the legal profession by an unqualified individual, or the omission to report a financial crime under the current legislation in Mauritius, or preventing a person from becoming a client of another law practitioner, etc.

builder might commit during the construction venture. It is deemed that the ten-year period is long enough so that all important defects in the building or in the land will be revealed, and the client may ask for compensation for all the harm stemming from those defects.

93. However, if there are apparent defects in the building or in the land on the day of the reception of works by the client, the latter has to object immediately to those defects; otherwise, the architect or the builder will not be liable for the harm suffered by the client. It will be considered that the client has accepted the apparent defects to which he or she has not objected.[146]

94. In the case Mauritius *Bholah H. v. The Training and Employment Persons Board* of 2004,[147] the issue that was raised was whether the action provided for in Article 1792 Civil Code was time-barred or not. After careful consideration, the Supreme Court reached the conclusion that the action was brought before a court on the last day of the ten-year period and that it was not time-barred.[148] In the case *Seenarain P. v. Govinda B.* of 2004,[149] it has been reminded that the ten-year period set out in Article 1792 Civil Code was of public interest (*d'ordre public*), meaning that the client and the builder/architect could not amend this period by contract.[150]However, the client and the builder/architect may make a transaction that will end any litigation even before it could start, preventing, thus, any potential action before a court of justice based on Article 1792 Civil Code. The obligation of the builder/architect to repair the harm suffered by the client is not of public interest, and its existence and scope may be defined in a private contract (*transaction*).

V. Notaries

95. In Mauritius, the duties and professional obligations of notaries are governed by the Notaries Act 2008. The Act sets out a certain number of duties, the violation of which constitutes a civil fault and may give rise to the notary's tort liability. For instance, section 3(3) of the Act imposes on notaries the obligation to keep in their custody every paper or electronic original drawn up or deposited. Section 3(4) of the Act adds that notaries have the duty to exercise their profession with impartiality and independence and to show loyalty and integrity towards the State, their

146. Cass. Civ 3, 22 Oct. 1974, Bull Civ III, No. 369.
147. 2004 SCJ 272.
148. According to the judgment, '(m)oreover, with regard to the computation of time in respect of Art. 2260 Civil Code "*Le jour où se produit l'événement qui lui sert de point de départ (die a quo) n'est pas compris dans le délai*". Consequently, learned Counsel for the respondent is quite right in submitting that the action of his client was not time barred as the plaint with summons was lodged on the last permissible day'.
149. 2004 SCJ 28.
150. According to the judgment, '(w)hen it is stated that the limitation of action of 10 years is a matter of public order, it simply means that the delay cannot be abridged by the parties. However, as regards the right of action, I am of the view that there is no prohibition for the parties to compromise as the obligation which the builder owes is not one of public order and any agreement to relinquish one's right of action would not be in breach of Article 2060 of the Civil Code'.

clients and other law practitioners. Notaries also have to keep professional secrecy and not divulge any of their clients' affairs except with their consent or when ordered to do so by a Court. Section 7 of the Act prohibits notaries from the acquisition of any interest in a matter in respect of which they provide their services; from the investment of any money received by them in their capacity of notary, whether or not interest is payable by them; from the reception or custody of any money on which the notary agrees to pay interest; from the signature of a notarial deed, a note or a receipt in blank, etc.[151] Section 8 of the Act contains some additional prohibitions for a notary. Notaries must not enter into a partnership or fee-sharing arrangement in relation to the exercise of the profession with a person who is not a notary; act as agent in any matter which can only be done by a notary for a person who is not a notary; or permit their name to be made use of in any matter on account or for the profit of a person who is not a notary. The prohibitions set out in sections 7 and 8 of the Act clearly aim to protect the image and impartiality of the important public office, which is the office of a notary. The same idea is behind section 34(1) of the Act: notaries shall keep accounts of all their receipts and expenditures, showing clearly and separately any amounts or securities received from or on behalf of their clients or returned or paid out. Section 34(3) adds that, in principle, when notaries receive a sum of money entrusted to them by or for a client, they shall, not later than twenty-one days after they receive the sum, deposit it in the client's account. The disciplinary proceedings against notaries are governed by section 36 of the Act.

Although the Supreme Court has not yet taken any decision on this point, we are of the view that the civil fault committed by notaries necessarily leads to their extra-contractual liability. Notaries are public officers providing public service to Mauritian citizens and residents.[152] They do not engage in a contractual relationship. This is why their civil liability is tortious and not a contractual one.

96. Even though the violation of a duty laid out in the Notaries Act 2008 clearly constitutes a civil fault, there is no doubt that a judge or a magistrate does not need to identify a specific provision of the Act before he or she reaches the conclusion that a notary has committed a civil fault and that he is liable in tort. There is a general duty not to harm others unjustly (*devoir de ne pas nuire injustement à autrui*) and the violation of this duty constitutes a civil fault under Articles 1382–1383 Civil Code. Thus, while assessing the behaviour of a notary, the civil Judge or the civil magistrate will apply the *in abstracto* test: is a notary's behaviour in line with what could have been expected in the same circumstances from a reasonable and careful notary with the same qualifications and the same experience. If the answer to this question is a negative one, the notary committed a civil fault, and he or she will be liable in tort.

---

151. Of course, notaries are not only public officers, but also citizens of Mauritius, which explains why s. 7(3) of the Act stipulates that nothing in the Law shall prevent a notary from borrowing any money for his personal needs on the security of his property. This kind of normal behaviour of a notary, in the course of his personal activities, cannot be considered a civil fault.

152. Noël Désiré Jean Pierre Michel, *La responsabilité civile des notaires* (Université de la Réunion/ Institute for Judicial and Legal Studies, 2018) 11–12; 15–23.

§2. Liability of Public Authorities

97. The tort liability of Mauritian public authorities, i.e., the Government of Mauritius and the organisms acting on behalf of the Mauritian State, is governed by the general rules on the liability for acts of others under Article 1384(3) Civil Code.[153] This has been reminded in the cases *DSA Company Ltd v. The Ministry of Public Infrastructure & Anor and Super Construction Co Ltd v. State of Mauritius* of 2013[154] and *Cundasamy v. the Government of Mauritius* of 2001. The application of this article stems from section 2(1) of the State Proceedings Act of 1953[155] which reads as follows: 'The State shall be subject to all those liabilities in tort to which, if it were a private person of full age and capacity, it would be subject in respect of torts committed by its employees or agents.' In other words, the tort liability of the Mauritian State and the organisms acting on behalf of the State will be applied if all main conditions for the application of the liability for acts of others according to Article 1384(3) Civil Code are satisfied. First, the claimant has to establish the civil liability of the employee or the agent acting on behalf of the State or on behalf of an organism representing the State. To do so, the claimant has to prove a civil fault giving rise to the personal tort liability of the employee or the agent of the State. This is clearly set out in section 2(1A) of the Act: 'No proceedings shall lie against the State (…) in respect of an act or omission of an employee or agent of the State, unless the act or omission would (…) have given rise to a cause of action in tort against that employee or agent or his estate.' Second, the claimant has to establish the subordination between the State or an organism acting on its behalf as the employer and the employee or the agent. Finally, the employee's or agent's fault has to be committed in the course of the fulfilment of his professional duties and missions.

98. It is noteworthy, however, that the liability of the State or the organisms acting on behalf of the State is not completely identical to the general regime of the liability for acts of others. First, section 4(1) and (2) of the Public Officers' Protection Act of 1957 stipulates that an action in tort against an employee of the State or the organism acting on behalf of the State will be time-barred after two years period and that procedural defence will be available to the State whose liability as principal is discussed before a court. Second, even though neither the Civil Code nor any other enactment requires that the civil fault of the employee is a gross one (*faute lourde*), the Supreme Court insists on that condition. In other words, only a gross civil fault may entail the tort liability of the State or of the organism acting on its behalf. This is clearly set out in the cases *Transpacific Export Services Ltd v. The State of Mauritius & Anor* of 2018[156] and 2016,[157] *Senarain v. The Commissioner of Police & Anor* of 2019[158] and *Mario Alain Chung Ching Ah Sue v. The State of*

153. *See* below para. 110.
154. 2013 SCJ 485.
155. Jonas Knetsch, *La réception du droit français de la responsabilité à Maurice*, RIDC 2017, 67–87, at paras 25–26.
156. 2018 UKPC 28.
157. 2016 SCJ 407.
158. 2019 SCJ 72.

Mauritius of 2015.[159] It has to be noted that gross civil fault is a flexible notion, which will be determined depending on the circumstances of a case.

99. It has also to be stressed that the tort liability of the public authorities in Mauritius as principal does not exclude the tort liability of the employees or the agents of those public authorities. The tort liability will be a joint one; the liability of the public authorities will be based on Article 1384 Civil Code, and the liability of the employee or the agent will result from Articles 1382–1383 of the same Code. The fact that there are two persons liable in tort gives an additional guarantee to the victim that his or her harm will be repaired.

100. There is no formal obstacle in Mauritius that once the tort liability of public authorities has been ascertained in a judgment, the compensation of the victims is done in kind and not through a sum of money paid to the victims of harm.

§3. Abuse of Rights

101. There is absolutely no doubt that the concept of abuse of rights forms part of the civil law of Mauritius. Thus, Article 16 Civil Code stipulates that 'everyone has the duty to use his rights and to fulfil his obligations in line with the requirements of good faith'. In addition, according to Article 17 'no one can use his rights with the intention to cause harm to other person or in a way that will cause to other person harm without proportion with the gain expected by the author of the act'.

102. It appears very clearly that several forms of abuse are explicitly prohibited under the tort law of Mauritius. The use of a right with the intention to cause harm to another person is a civil fault. Even though there is no such intention, a behaviour may be considered an abuse of rights and, thus, a civil fault, if there is recklessness in the use of a right. An example is given in Article 17 Civil Code: the lack of proportion between the harm suffered by a victim and the gain expected by the author of the act. Other forms of abuse may also exist, even though they are not explicitly mentioned in Articles 16 and 17 of the Code, such as the contradiction in the behaviour of the author of an act, the total unusefulness of the act, etc. In the cases *Gendoo v. Razbully* of 2010[160] and *Hurloll Leelder v. Choolun Anandissan* of 2007,[161] civil fault resulted from a misuse of the right to report an offence committed to the public authorities. In those two cases, the misuse of the above-mentioned right was motivated by the intention of the tortfeasor to take vengeance against the victim of a false report to the public authorities on an offence allegedly committed by the latter.

159. 2015 SCJ 110.
160. 2010 INT 149.
161. 2007 INT 85.

103. The case *Sewraz Frères Ltd v. Nestlé Products (Mauritius) Ltd* of 2014[162] pertained to a contract made by two companies by virtue of which one of them had the right to distribute in Mauritius the products of the other as of 1 January 1991. In July 1995, the supplier informed the distributor that he wished to put an end to the above-mentioned distribution contract as of 31 October 1995. It was stipulated in the contract that it could be ended subject to the respect of a three-month notice period. This is exactly what the supplier did, and the distributor failed to prove that the unilateral decision of the supplier to put an end to the contract with the distributor was a source of an abuse of rights.

104. In the case *Cascadelle Distribution et Cie Ltée v. Nestlé Products* of 2015,[163] the Supreme Court reminded that a misuse of a right stemming from the contract constitutes a civil fault and may entail the application of the tort liability of the author of that misuse. For instance, the unilateral decision to put an end to a contract of indeterminate duration without giving the other contractual party a sufficient notice period will be regarded as an abuse of rights. The abuse of a right may also result from the lack of effort of the party that puts an end to the contract to listen to the arguments of the other party and to try to find a solution to maintain the contract in force.

§4. Injury to Reputation and Privacy

105. To our best knowledge, there are no specific rules on civil fault pertaining to an injury to the reputation and privacy of natural and juristic persons. Such an injury may be considered a source of civil fault if the *in abstracto* test has been satisfied. For instance, a lie that is detrimental to the claimant's reputation will be considered a civil fault, entailing the application of the tort liability of the defendant. Moreover, if an individual makes an unauthorised revelation pertaining to the sexual orientation or personal relationship of another individual, the latter may claim damages from the former as such a behaviour constitutes a civil fault.

106. In the case *Nazir Ahmad Bukhuth v. Tejnarain Chumroo* of 2018,[164] the Intermediate Court held that the defendant had committed a civil fault by defamatory remarks, as he made 'the gratuitous allegations and accusations' against the claimant 'which caused him to be transferred until matters be sorted out and enquiry be conducted'.

107. Upon a review of the law of defamation as applicable in Mauritius, the Court went on to say that the English law of libel was not the law of Mauritius, but that guidance might be sought from English authorities and case law on the subject where the principles applicable to any issue involved were the same in the French

162. 2014 SCJ 157.
163. 2015 SCJ 120.
164. 2018 INT 28.

and English systems. In the case *Dookhony v. La Sentinelle Ltd & Anor of 2008*,[165] quoted as an authority, it was held that 'defamatory imputations have been established, they are presumed to have been made with intention to cause harm, hence a presumption of *faute* so that the burden would shift on the defendant to prove his good faith'.

§5. Interference by a Third Person with Contractual Relations

108. Under the law of Mauritius, there is a well-established principle of relative effect of a contract (*effet relatif du contrat*), according to which the contract will generate rights and obligations only for the contracting parties. The obligatory force of the contract (*force obligatoire du contrat*) stipulated in Article 1134 Civil Code prevents both parties to the contract from doing anything that might imperil the proper fulfilment of the contractual duties. It means that the contract may be opposed by all third parties. From the point of view of those third parties, the contract is a social fact that has to be taken into account and respected. Those third parties have to restrain from doing anything that might hinder the proper execution of the contract. For instance, Article 1141 Civil Code stipulates that the second buyer of a movable property whose purchase contract has been made after the first one made between the owner and the first buyer will be protected and considered owner of the goods, provided that the second buyer has acted in good faith and that the object has been handed to him. In other words, if the second buyer of a movable property has acted in good faith and did not know that there was a first buyer of the same movable property to whom the owner did not hand the object, the second buyer will be considered owner of the object as from the moment he receives the possession of it. However, if the second buyer was aware of the existence of the first purchase agreement between the owner and a different buyer to which the object of purchase has not been handed, this first buyer will be considered owner of the object.

109. This exception is based on the principle *fraus omnia corrumpit*.[166] In other words, the fact that the second buyer has bought an object and received it from the seller in spite of the knowledge of the existence of the purchase contract between the seller (owner) and the first buyer will constitute a civil fault. Consequently, the contract between the second buyer and the owner will not be opposable to the first buyer. Similar principles apply to two different purchase contracts of immovable property, such as a house or a plot of land, made one after another between the owner and two different buyers. The legal situation of the first buyer can be compared, in principle, to two different purchase contracts made by the owner of a movable property with two different buyers. Thus, the existence and the contents of the immovable property rights are easily established thanks to a register kept by the Conservator of mortgages (*conservateur des hypothèques*). Every buyer of an immovable property may transcribe his rights stemming from a notarial deed in the

165. 2008 SCJ 61.
166. It means that fraud vitiates everything.

register. From that point, it becomes very simple to prove that the first buyer of an immovable property, who has transcribed his right in the appropriate register of the Conservator, did not do anything wrong and that he will be considered owner of the immovable property. His right will be opposable to the second buyer of the same property.However, if the second buyer transcribes his right in the register of the Conservator of mortgages before the first one does so, the second buyer will be considered owner. However, in line with the core principle *fraus omnia corrumpit*, if the second buyer who registered his right first knew that the same immovable property had been bought by a first buyer who has not registered his right yet, the latter will be considered owner. Those principles stem from the cases *Soobramanien v. Jogoo & Ors* of 2007,[167] *Beerjeeraz & Ors v. Dabee M. A.* of 2010[168] and *Nursimloo v. Etwa & Ors* of 2002.[169] The fact that the second buyer knew the existence of the first one, who bought the same property earlier, corrupts the legal title of the second buyer. In those circumstances, the registration of the ownership title of the second buyer in the register of the Conservator of Mortgage is considered an act of bad faith and a civil fault. The sanction, the non-opposability of the second purchase agreement to the first buyer, is a sort of reparation in kind (*réparation en nature*).

167. 2007 SCJ 36.
168. 2010 SCJ 11.
169. 2002 SCJ 222.

Part II. Liability for Acts of Others

Chapter 1. Vicarious Liability

110. Vicarious liability is defined as the 'liability that a supervisory party (…) bears for the actionable conduct of a subordinate or associate (…) based on the relationship between the two parties'.[170] In other words, 'it represents not a tort, but a rule of responsibility which renders the defendant liable for the torts committed by another'.[171]

111. Under Article 1384(3) Civil Code, an employer is vicariously liable for the tortious acts of its employees, provided that those acts have been committed 'in the course of employment' (*dans les fonctions auxquelles ils sont employés*). Paragraph 2 of the same Article stipulates that the father and the mother are liable in tort and *in solido* as long as they exercise the parental authority together for the harm caused by their minor child living with them. Article 1384(4) adds that teachers are liable for the harm caused by a pupil while the latter is under the supervision of the former. The same rule applies to the harm caused by an apprentice.

112. Section 160 of the Companies Act of 2001[172] deals with the standard of care and civil liability of officers, including directors of a company.

§1. Employee/Employer

113. Article 1384(3) Civil Code stipulates that the principals are vicariously liable in tort for the harm caused by their agents in the fulfilment of their functions.[173] The function mentioned in this text encompasses a series of tasks of similar nature.

114. This brief definition reveals the existence of three main conditions for the application of the vicarious liability of the principal, namely the preposition link

170. https://www.law.cornell.edu/wex/vicarious_liability (last visited on 30 Jun. 2024).
171. Paula Giliker, *Vicarious Liability in Tort. A Comparative Perspective* (CUP 2010) 1.
172. Act 15/2001.
173. *See Acms Ltd v. Blencowe* [2019 SCJ 179].

(*lien de préposition*),[174] a fault committed by the agent,[175] and the sufficient link between the agent's fault and his or her functions.[176]

I. Preposition Link

115. The preposition link traditionally means that the principal has the power to give orders to the agent, to decide on the manner in which those orders will be carried out, and to closely control the respect and proper execution of the aforesaid order.[177] This definition of *préposition* is borrowed from the French Law and, in particular, from the *Société Générale* case of 1996,[178] given the fact that, in Mauritius, the contract law is of French inspiration and that contract is the main source of the preposition link. French Civil Law and especially the judgments of the French Court of cassation are the persuasive authority for Mauritian Civil Law.[179]

116. However, a contract is not the only source of a preposition link, even though it is the main one. If a contract creates the subordination link, the power to give orders to the agent is a legal one, based on a legal instrument named contract. The preposition link may also be generated by a factual situation and the power to give orders may thus be a factual one. This happens when an individual gives a helping hand to a friend or a close relative, acts under his orders, and during the fulfilment of his functions, that individual commits a fault and causes harm to a third person. For instance, an individual is driving a truck in order to help a friend and, due to lack of concentration, causes physical and moral harm to a pedestrian. The latter will be allowed to bring an action before a court against the friend benefiting from the help of the tortfeasor as the former qualifies as principal.

117. The main source of the preposition link in Mauritius is employment contracts. Traditionally, it is said that the employment contract creates the preposition link because the employer has the legal power (based on the employment contract) to give orders to his employees, to decide on the manner in which the orders will be

174. *See*, under French law, for example François Terré, Philippe Simler, Yves Lequette & François Chénedé, *Droit civil – Les obligations* (Dalloz, 12th ed. 2019) paras 1160–1162; Porchy-Simon, *supra* n. 131, at paras 830–832.

175. Porchy-Simon, *supra* n. 131, at paras 833–834; Terré, Simler, Lequette & Chénédé, *supra* n. 175, at paras 1063–1064.

176. Porchy-Simon, *supra* n. 131, at paras 835–843.

177. *See*, under French law, for example Emmanuel Dockès, Gilles Auzero & Dirk Baugard, *Droit du travail* (Dalloz, 35th ed. 2021) para. 200.

178. Cass. Soc., 13 Nov. 1996, No. 94-13187.

179. *See Lingel-Roy v. The State of Mauritius* [2017 SCJ 411]: 'It is appropriate to recall the practice that when it comes to the interpretation of a law borrowed from French law we stand guided for its interpretation by French doctrine and case law. One can quote in that respect the following passage from *L'Etendry v. The Queen* [1953 MR 15]: "the normal rule of construction laid down time and again by this court (...) is to the effect that when our law is borrowed from French law we should resort for guidance as to its interpretation to French doctrine and case law." But, it has to be pointed out that the practice of relying on French authorities has always been for guidance and not in application of the stare decisis principle.'

carried out and to closely control the fulfilment of those orders. For instance, a gardening company has the contractual right to give orders to its employees, to decide on the best way to fulfil their missions and functions and to closely control the executions of the orders given to them. If necessary, disciplinary action will be taken against the employee. This traditional definition of the subordination link has been given in the case *Dassruth v. Femi Publishing Co Ltd & Ors* of 2016.[180]

118. It needs to be noted that this traditional definition of the preposition link does not fit well with some employment contracts made with highly skilled employees such as doctors, informaticians, teachers, etc. In those professions, it is difficult or impossible for the employer to give orders on the technical aspects of the employee's everyday missions and to closely control their fulfilment, as employees in those professions keep an important degree of autonomy in the execution of their everyday tasks. This is why the power to apply disciplinary measures against the employees becomes the main criterion in such cases in order to ascertain whether the subordination link exists or not. The other important criteria in such types of situations is the power of the employer to determine the place and the time of the employee's activity.

II. Employee's Civil Fault

119. The second condition of the application of the employer's liability is that the employee's acts and omissions must qualify as fault. It is true that Article 1384 Civil Code does not mention this condition explicitly, but this is the only reasonable interpretation. How could an employer be liable in tort for the employee's acts and omissions when the employee has not committed any civil fault? It would not make any sense.[181] This second condition has been clearly set out in the cases *Gowry v. The State* of 1996[182] and *Vikas Trading Co Ltd v. The Government of Mauritius* of 2001.[183] In the case *Jhugdamby v. Private Secondary Education Authority* of 2022, the Supreme Court clearly asserts that '(h)owever, to engage the vicarious liability of the principal, it is necessary to prove fault on the part of the direct author of the damages, i.e., the agent, committed in the performance of his duties'.[184]

III. Sufficient Link Between Agent's Fault and his Functions

120. An employer will be liable in tort for the civil faults committed by his or her employee only when there is a sufficient link between the employee's (agent's) fault and his or her functions. More precisely, the employee's fault must be committed in the course of the fulfilment of his or her functions as an employee. For

180. 2016 SCJ 56.
181. Porchy-Simon, *supra* n. 131, at paras 833–834; Terré, Simler, Lequette & Chénédé, *supra* n. 175, at paras 1063–1064.
182. 1996 SCJ 135.
183. 2001 SCJ 237.
184. 2022 SCJ 56.

example, if a negligent employee causes a road accident while he or she is transporting the employer's goods and during office hours and hurts a pedestrian, the employer will be liable in tort for the physical and moral harm suffered by the pedestrian. This is due to the existence of a sufficient link between the employee's fault and the fulfilment of the employee's mission, as the latter was carried out during office hours, in the best interest of the employer and with a means (vehicle) provided by the employer.

121. However, in some cases, doubts may exist as to whether the employee's fault has been linked enough to his functions. This may happen when the employee commits a civil fault at the workplace, during office hours and using the means provided by the employer but is not acting in the employer's best interest but rather in his or her purely personal interest. This is known as abuse of functions (*abus de fonctions*).

122. As already explained,[185] French Civil Law and especially the judgments of the Court of Cassation play in Mauritius the role of a persuasive authority, meaning that the Mauritian courts may follow the legal reasoning expressed in it but do not have any legal obligation to do so.

123. In a 1988 case,[186] the Court of Cassation laid out three very clear criteria that have been defined in order to answer the question of the tort liability of an employer for the abuse of functions committed by his employee. The employer will not be liable for the employee's actions when those actions are disconnected from the employee's usual missions, are not approved by the employer and are taken in a purely personal interest of the employee.[187] For instance, if a company's driver uses a company's car to drive his children to school, it is obvious that his action does not fit his usual missions and functions, which are to drive the people and goods in the best interest of his company. When the driver provokes a road accident and causes moral and material harm to a third party, the company – the driver's employer – will not be liable in tort for the loss caused by its driver, given that the organs of the company have never approved that the driver uses the official car to drive his children to school and that the action has been taken in the exclusive interest of the driver. When a petrol truck driver tries to transfer a part of the cargo that he is transporting with the intention to embezzle it, and while doing so, he causes material harm to a third party, the company employing the truck driver will not be liable in tort for the action of the latter, as this action has nothing to do with the normal functions of the truck driver (driving the goods for the benefit of the company), has been taken without the companies prior or a *posteriori* approval and has been taken in order to procure to the driver personal and illegal gain (the value of the embezzled petrol).

---

185. *See* para. 46 above.
186. Cass. Ass. plén., 17 Jun. 1988, No. 87-85018.
187. Porchy-Simon, *supra* n. 131, at para. 837.

124. The Mauritian Supreme Court has transposed those three criteria into the tort law of Mauritius. In the case *Dookhy & Ors v. SBM,*[188] it held that a bank-employer had not been liable in tort for the civil fault of an employee who had embezzled for his own personal benefit a part of the loan granted to a client. The bank had never ordered or approved such an action, and the aforesaid action does not form part of the bank employee's missions and functions. The only person liable in tort is the employee who committed this civil fault. The aforesaid criteria have been confirmed in the case *Beau Villa v. Chuckowree and Lamco Insurance Ltd* of 1992.[189] In this case, an employer was held vicariously liable in tort for the harm caused by his employer in the course of his employment. The employee had acted without the prior consent of his employer, but the former did not act to satisfy an objective exterior to his missions and functions.

125. For a long time, there was no Mauritian case law as to the nature of the employer's liability, i.e., whether his liability for his employee's torts committed in the course of the fulfilment of his duties was a subjective one, and based on the employer's fault, or an objective (strict) one, completely independent of any idea of employer's fault. The first possible solution is to hold the employer subjectively liable for his employee's civil faults and to presume that the employer has committed a civil fault while he was choosing his employee or while he was supervising him. This interpretation provides employers with the possibility to avoid civil liability by proving that they have properly chosen their employees and that they have been properly supervising them. The second possible solution is that the employer's liability is strict, which means that the employer cannot escape from it without proving a case of force majeure,[190] excluding both the employee's and the employer's liability.[191] This solution is based on the idea that the employee's activity is economically beneficial for the employer, that it is fair and just, and that the latter supports the risk of negative economic consequences that the employee could cause to third parties. The objective (strict) liability of the employer has been clearly set out in the case *Jhugdamby v. Private Secondary Education Authority* of 2022. According to this judgment, '(i)n respect of vicarious liability of the principal it is objective and strict, i.e., "*no fault liability*". It means that there is no need to prove fault on the part of the principal'.[192]

126. One of the practically very important issues in the tort law of Mauritius is the issue of the employee's and employer's parallel liability, i.e., the issue of the employee's and employer's solidary liability. Under French tort law, the employer's civil liability normally excludes the employee's personal civil liability, the employee benefitting from a liability immunity provided that he or she did not commit an intentional criminal or civil fault. This solution stems from the French cases

188. 2007 SCJ 1.
189. 1992 SCJ 83.
190. In this context, the force majeure may be defined as an external event, reasonably unforeseeable and whose consequences are reasonably inevitable.
191. *See*, under French law, Jacques Flour, Jean-Luc Aubert & Eric Savaux, *Droit civil – Les obligations*, vol. 2 *Le fait juridique* (Sirey, 14th ed. 2011) paras 205 and 207.
192. 2022 SCJ 56.

Costedoat of 2000[193] and *Cousin* of 2001.[194] The Supreme Court has not followed the French Law on this particular point. Mauritian case law does not exclude the tort liability of the employee when the employer is vicariously liable. This solution was set out in the cases *Vikas Trading Co Ltd v. The Government of Mauritius*[195] and *Beau Villa v. Chuckowree and Lamco Insurance Ltd.*[196] It means that when an employer is vicariously liable, he or she and his or her employee will be liable *in solido* for the harm caused to a third party by the employee. The aggrieved third party will have the choice to ask for the integral compensation of his harm, either by the employer or by the employee. The choice will, of course, depend on the solvency of the employer and the employee. In general, the former is more solvent than the latter, and the victim of the harm caused by the employee will usually bring an action before a court of justice not against the employee but against the employer.

§2. Independent Contractors

127. Even though the contract for service is not defined in Articles 1780 and the subsequent Civil Code, it can be defined as a contract according to which a person called an independent contractor (*entrepreneur*) promises to carry out physical or intellectual work[197] for another person called client (*maître de l'ouvrage*) and the latter needs to pay to the former a remuneration for the aforesaid work.[198] The major difference between an employment contract and a contract for services is that the independent contractor is *legally* independent in the organisation and the execution of the work ordered by his client. In other words, the client does not give orders to the independent contractor on how to carry out his mission, does not decide on the way in which the mission will be executed and does not apply the disciplinary sanctions against the independent contractor. It means that there is no subordination between both parties, and it prevents the client from being vicariously liable in tort for the actions of the independent contractor. Article 1384(3) does not apply to the relationship between the client and the independent contractor.

128. It may happen that a contractor legally independent from the client is yet economically dependent. For instance, a small enterprise might be economically dependent on a large-scale enterprise, which is delegating to this small enterprise, on a regular basis, a part of the work to be carried out for the benefit of the client. In spite of this economic dependence, the client (large-scale enterprise) will not be vicariously liable in tort for the actions of the economically dependent contractor,

193. Cass Ass plén, 25 Feb. 2000, No. 97-17378.
194. Cass Ass plén, 14 Dec. 2001, No. 00-82066.
195. 2001 SCJ 237.
196. 1992 SCJ 83.
197. *See*, under French law, Deen Gibirila, *Louage d'ouvrage et d'industrie. Contrat d'entreprise*, JurisClasseur Code Civil, Art. 1787, Fasc 10, 2014, para. 2.
198. Cass Civ 1, 19 Feb. 1968, Bull Civ 1968, I, No. 69; Cass Com, 2 Nov. 1965, Bull Civ 1965, III, No. 546; Cass Civ 1, 19 Mar. 1968, Bull Civ 1968, I, No. 106; Cass Civ 3, 26 Apr. 1972, No. 70-14043; Bull Civ 1972, III, No. 262. *See also* Joseph Frossard, *La distinction des obligations de moyens et des obligations de résultat* (LGDJ 1965).

given the fact that the preposition link, which is one of the conditions of the vicarious liability, has to be of legal and not of economic nature. This has clearly been stated in the French case *Bardou* of 1931,[199] which is a persuasive authority for Mauritian Law.

§3. Liability of Legal Entities for Acts of their Organs

129. Section 160(1) of the Companies Act 2001 stipulates that every officer of a company must carry out his professional duties and powers 'honestly, in good faith and in the best interests of the company'. His or her behaviour needs to reflect 'the degree of care, diligence and skill that a reasonably prudent person would exercise in comparable circumstances'.

130. This definition of the standard of care of a company's officers perfectly matches the general definition of civil fault. As already mentioned in the Chapter on Liability for One's Own Acts,[200] the assessment of fault is done *in abstracto*,[201] which means that the defendant's behaviour is compared to what is expected of an average and careful individual under the same circumstances. The model of reference is an abstract 'average and careful individual', here, an abstract average and careful officer of a company. The *in abstracto* test has been applied in the cases *Neron Publications Co Ltd v. La Sentinelle Ltd & Ors* of 2020,[202] *Hurnam v. Dabee* of 2010,[203] *Belloguet & Anor v. Mungur & Ors* of 2019,[204] *Cundasawmy v. The Government of Mauritius* of 2001[205] and *Ungnoo & Anor v. State of Mauritius* of 2005.[206]

131. However, the defendant's occupation is taken into account while the *in abstracto* test is applied. A judge or a magistrate will need to ascertain whether the defendant has done everything that a careful person having the same professional qualification and the same experience – here, an average and careful officer of a company having the same professional qualification and the same experience – would have done under identical circumstances. If the answer is a positive one, the defendant (the officer of a company) has not committed a civil fault and will not be liable in tort.However, if the answer to the above question is no, the defendant will be held liable.

132. More specifically, section 160(4) of the Companies Act 2001 stipulates that a director or other officer of a company must make a business judgment in good

199. *Dalloz Périodique*, 1931, 1, 131. *See also* Dockès, Auzero & Baugard, *supra* n. 178, at para. 203.
200. *See* paras 76–77 above.
201. *See*, under French law, Porchy-Simon, *supra* n. 131, at para. 798.
202. 2020 SCJ 63.
203. 2010 INT 244.
204. 2019 SCJ 218.
205. 2001 SCJ 69; 2001 MR 25.
206. 2005 SCJ 89.

faith for a proper purpose, avoid any conflict of interest, inform the company of the business judgment to the extent he or she reasonably believes to be appropriate and act in the best interest of the company.

133. The truth is that most of the time, a director or other officer of a private company vested with managing powers enters into contracts with third parties on behalf of his company. In case a director or other officer vested with managing powers commits a civil fault in the discharge of his duties and powers while executing a contract on behalf of a company, the company's liability for its director's wrongdoings will be a contractual one. Indeed, under the law of Mauritius, contractual liability is defined in Article 1147 Civil Code as the liability for the inexecution or bad execution of contractual duties and obligations. However, a civil fault committed by the director of a private company before entering into a contract with a third party and on behalf of the company will lead to the extra-contractual liability of the company for the wrongdoings of the director. For instance, if the director's fault is committed during the negotiation phase[207] or while exercising a contractual prerogative to put an end to the contract unilaterally,[208] it is generally considered that this fault, preceding the conclusion and execution of the contract, gives rise to a liability in tort and not in contract. The company will be vicariously liable in tort for the fault committed by its director in accordance with Article 1384(3) Civil Code.

134. It also has to be noted that in Mauritius, the vicarious liability in tort of the State and the state and parastatal organisations for the torts committed by their employees is governed by Article 1384(3) Civil Code.[209] The application of this text is provided for by section 2(1) of the State Proceedings Act 1953.[210] This has been reminded in the cases *DSA Company Ltd v. The Ministry of Public Infrastructure & Anor* and *Super Construction Co Ltd v. State of Mauritius* of 2013[211] and *Cundasamy v. The Government of Mauritius* of 2001.[212] There is, however, an important specificity of this vicarious tort liability of the State and parastatal organisations for the torts committed by their employees, as provided in section 4(1) of the Public Officers' Protection Act of 1957, compared to the general rules laid out in the Civil Code. An action in tort brought against a State's employee or a state and parastatal organisations' employee will be time-barred after two years from the moment the tort (civil fault) has been committed, instead of ten years.[213] This has been clearly stated in the case *Ancharaz v. State of Mauritius* of 2011.[214] Moreover, according to section 2(4) of the State Proceedings Act, this time-related defence (two years) is also available to the State and parastatal organisations whose employee has committed a tort (civil fault) in the discharge of his or her duties. In other words, the

207. *See*, under French law, Terré, Simler, Lequette & Chénédé, *supra* n. 175, at para. 240.
208. *Cascadelle Distribution et Cie Ltée v. Nestle Products* [2015 SCJ 120].
209. *See* paras 97–100 above.
210. *See* Knetsch, *supra* n. 156, at paras 25–26.
211. 2013 SCJ 485.
212. 2001 SCJ 60.
213. Article 2270 Civil Code.
214. 2011 SCJ 189.

State and parastatal organisations will not be vicariously liable in tort for the torts committed by their employees in the fulfilment of their duties, if the victim brings an action in tort before a court of justice more than two years after the tort has been committed. There is another specificity of the vicarious liability in tort of the State: very often, Mauritian Courts require that the civil fault committed by the employee must be a gross one (*faute lourde*); otherwise, the state and parastatal organisations will not be liable. This has been clearly indicated in the cases *Transpacific Export Services Ltd v. The State of Mauritius* of 2018[215] and 2016,[216] *Senarain v. The Commissioner of Police* of 2019[217] and *Mario Alain Chung Ching Ah Sue v. The State of Mauritius* of 2015.[218] In the more recent case *Jhugdamby v. Private Secondary Education Authority* of 2022, the Supreme Court stated that '(a)s regards the administrative tort liability, the public authority as principal is liable for the acts committed by its agents only to the extent that it has been done in bad faith or amounts to a *faute lourde*'.[219] This requirement is very protective of the Mauritian State and its financial interests, as this makes it difficult to declare the State liable for the torts committed by its employees. The proof of a *faute lourde* committed by the employee is not easy to provide before a court of justice. However, one may notice that the vicarious tort liability of Mauritian public hospitals for the civil faults committed by its employees does not require that the civil fault of the employee is a gross one: a simple civil fault of negligence or imprudence committed by an employee of the public hospital will entail the vicarious tort liability of the latter. This is clearly set out in the cases *Belloguet & Anor v. Mungur & Ors* of 2019[220] and *Cundasamy v. The Government of Mauritius* of 2001.[221]

215. 2018 UKPC 28.
216. 2016 SCJ 407.
217. 2019 SCJ 72.
218. 2015 SCJ 110.
219. 2022 SCJ 56.
220. 2019 SCJ 218.
221. 2001 SCJ 60 ('It is interesting to note that in France the jurisprudence in respect of "la responsabilité médicale" has evolved in favour of the patient from "faute lourde" to "faute simple".').

Chapter 2. Liability of Parents & Teachers

135. According to Article 1384(2) Civil Code, a father and a mother, as long as they exercise the guardianship over their child, are liable in tort *in solido* for all the harm caused by their minor child living with them to third parties. There are two possible interpretations as to the nature of the civil liability of parents: a subjective one, based on the civil fault committed by the parents, or an objective one (strict liability), that is regardless of any fault committed by the parents.

136. The Supreme Court of Mauritius has not departed from the first interpretation, as it arises directly from the Civil Code provisions. Parents are liable for the harm caused by their minor child, except when they can prove that they have properly educated their child and that they have properly monitored him or her. In other words, the parents will be exonerated from their tort liability if they succeed in proving that they have not committed any civil fault related to the child's behaviour. This solution was applied in the case *Rabaille v. Boodhun* of 1978.[222] A 17-year-old boy has wounded a client of the bakery where the boy was working at the time. The victim brought an action before the Supreme Court, claiming that the boy's parents be held liable under Article 1384(2) Civil Code. The Court rejected this claim as the parents have proven that they had properly educated and monitored their 17-year-old son.

137. The second solution, i.e., the strict (objective) liability of the parents, is applied in French law which, as already explained before, plays the role of a persuasive authority in Mauritius. Since the *Bertrand* case of 1997,[223] the Court of Cassation has not allowed parents to prove that they have properly educated or monitored their minor child in order to escape their liability. The only legal way for the parents to avoid their liability is to prove that the harm has been caused by a force majeure and not by the fault of their minor child. This second solution is based on the idea that the strict liability of the parents is the price to pay for the legal and factual power that the parents exercise over their minor child. However, the Supreme Court of Mauritius has not yet applied this solution, which is more severe for the parents as it becomes more difficult for them to avoid their tort liability.

138. According to Article 1384(2) Civil Code, there are four conditions for the civil liability of the parents: the parental authority over the child, the child's minority (§2), the living under the same roof (*cohabitation*) (§3) and the child's fault (§4).

§1. The Guardianship (*Droit de Garde*) Over the Child

139. Article 1384(2) Civil Code and the presumption of fault provided for in this text are applicable only to a father or/and a mother as long as they exercise guardianship over the child.[224] In any other case, the liability of a person who educates

222. 1978 MR 34.
223. Cass Civ 2, 19 Feb. 1997, No. 94-21111.
224. Pascal Ancel, *Droit des obligations en 12 thèmes* (Dalloz, 2nd ed. 2020) 469.

the child temporarily or monitors the child is based on the proof of a civil fault of that person, in line with Articles 1382–1383 Civil Code. In this above-mentioned situation, the civil fault is not presumed and must be proven. For instance, if the harm was caused by a child staying with his grand-parents, the grand-parents may be held liable only if the claimant proves that they have committed a civil fault. The same principle applies if the harm to a third party has been caused while the child was staying in a recreational institution.

140. When the parents are married, they exercise both guardianship over the child,[225] which means that they are liable *in solido*[226] for the harm caused by their minor child and their liability is based on a presumption of their civil fault (the lack of education or the lack of monitoring of their child). The same solution applies when the parents are not married, but they recognise the child, live together under the same roof, and exercise guardianship rights over their minor child.[227]However, in some cases, only one parent exercises the guardianship rights over the child and the other does not. This may happen in case of divorce[228] or when the parents are not married and do not live together.[229] In those cases, only the parent who exercises the guardianship rights over the child will be liable in tort. The other parent who is vested with visitation rights may be declared liable in tort for the harm caused by his minor child during the exercise of the visitation rights, but only if this parent's fault is proven (the lack of education or the lack of monitoring of their child), according to Articles 1382 and 1383 Civil Code. In this case, the parent's fault will not be presumed, as Article 1384(2) does not apply.

§2. THE MINORITY OF THE CHILD

141. The tort liability of the parents based on Article 1384(2) Civil Code only applies if the child was a minor at the time of the loss. In Mauritius, the age of minority is eighteen years.[230] However, it is not necessary that the child is still a minor at the moment when the judgment has been made in order to repair the harm to the victim.

§3. THE LIVING UNDER THE SAME ROOF (*COHABITATION*)

142. According to Article 1384(2) Civil Code, the parents and their minor child need to live under the same roof at the moment the harm is caused. This is a very

225. Article 372 Civil Code.
226. This means that defendants may choose the parent against which they will bring an action before a court and ask that the defendant compensate them for the whole harm suffered. In general, the action will be brought by the parent who is financially stronger.
227. Article 374 Civil Code.
228. Articles 373-2 and 261 Civil Code.
229. Article 374 Civil Code.
230. Article 388 Civil Code.

logical condition because living under the same roof gives the parents the opportunity to educate and monitor their children well. And if they do not, one can presume that they commit a civil fault and are liable in tort in conformity with Article 1384 paragraph 2 of the Mauritian Civil Code.[231]

§4. A Civil Fault Committed by the Child

143. Parents are liable in tort under Article 1384(2) Civil Code only if the action of the child qualifies as a civil fault according to Articles 1382–1383 Civil Code. This requirement is also a very logical one because it would be very difficult to understand the liability in tort of the parents where the child did not commit any civil fault.[232]

144. It has to be noted that the liability of the parents, based on Article 1384(2) Civil Code, does not exclude the child's personal liability. Since the case *Medine Sugar Estates Co Ltd v. Anthony* of 1990,[233] even minor children without the capacity of discernment may commit a civil fault and be liable for it.[234] However, in practice, it will be very rare that the victim brings an action against a minor because, very often, the child will not possess sufficient financial resources to compensate the victim.

§5. Liability of Teachers

145. Article 1384(4) Civil Code stipulates that teachers are liable in tort for the harm that their students could cause to third parties while the students are monitored by their teachers. The civil liability of teachers is a subjective one under the law of Mauritius, based on *faute*. This fault is reflected by the lack of monitoring or the insufficient monitoring of the students. Given the fact that there is a special rule for the tort liability of the teachers and that Articles 1382–1383 Civil Code are not applicable to this situation, we consider that the civil fault of the teacher is necessarily presumed and that the teacher will be exonerated from his or her tort liability for the student's action, if the former proves that he or she has properly monitored the latter.

231. Cass Civ 1, 2 Jul. 1991, Bull Civ I, No. 224; Cass Civ 2, 24 Apr. 1989, D 1990, 519.
232. *See also* Cass Civ 2, 10 May 2001, Bull Civ II, No. 96.
233. 1990 SCJ 334.
234. *See* paras 73 and 79 above.

Part III. Forms of Strict Liability

Chapter 1. Liability for Things and Animals

146. In Mauritius, a general regime of the liability for things is established in Article 1384 Civil Code. Paragraph 5 of this text stipulates that the guardian of a thing is liable for the harm caused by a thing, and according to paragraph 6, the guardian will be exonerated of his tort liability if the harm stems from a force majeure or from an exclusive civil fault of the victim.

147. Under the law of Mauritius, liability for things is an objective (strict) one, which means that guardians cannot be exonerated by proving that they did not commit any civil fault or that the loss is a result of an internal defect of the thing. It has to be noted that under French law, the liability of the guardian for the harm caused by things was introduced in 1930 in the famous *Jand'heur* case.[235] This liability regime has been created by an innovative interpretation by the Court of Cassation on the basis of Article 1384(1) Civil Code. In 1804, this provision was simply an introduction without any normative value, but in 1930, the judges used this text to introduce a new strict liability regime. In 1937, the Mauritian judges had a perfect opportunity to follow the position set out in the *Jand'heur* case and to introduce the same principle in Mauritius. In the famous case *Mangroo v. Dahal* of 1937,[236] an individual died due to an internal defect in a car, and the victim's heirs asked the Supreme Court to declare the owner of the car strictly liable. However, the Supreme Court has clearly expressed the position that its role was not to create the laws but to apply them and that the strict liability of the guardian for the harm caused by things needed to be provided for in a law.[237] It was not until 1983 that paragraphs 5 and 6 of Article 1384 providing for the objective (strict) liability of the guardian were introduced in the Mauritian Civil Code,[238] and the first important case pertaining to this new type of tort liability was the case of *Rose Belle SE Board v. Chateauneuf Ltd* of 1990.[239] Since then, the strict liability of the guardian for the harm caused by the thing is a well-established principle.

235. Cass Ch réunies, 13 Feb. 1930, Bulletin Arrêts Cour de Cassation Chambres réunies, n° 34, p. 68.
236. 1937 MR 43.
237. According to the judgment, '(t)he interpretation given to Article 1384-1 in *Jand'heur* by the Court of Cassation was contrary to the text and to the spirit and intention of the legislator and […] by so doing the French Judges had usurped the role of the legislator'.
238. Act 9/1983.
239. 1990 MR 9 and 16.

§1. CONDITIONS OF THE STRICT LIABILITY FOR THE HARM CAUSED BY THINGS

148. First of all, there has to be a thing, i.e., an object that has an owner who uses it, controls it and monitors it. Things that have no master (*res nullius*) do not fall within the scope of Article 1384 Civil Code, as there is no one who can be considered their guardian. For instance, Article 1384(5) and (6) of the Code does not apply to wild animals in the open space as no one owns them and no one monitors them.

149. Article 1384(5) and (6) Civil Code apply without any distinction to both movable and immovable property,[240] except domestic animals, for which there is a special rule in Article 1385 Civil Code and the buildings that are dealt with in Article 1386 Civil Code. Thus, Article 1384 applies to a vast array of movable things, such as cars, gas bottles, laptops, TV screens, etc. and to immovable things, such as plots of land.However, Article 1384 Civil Code does not take into consideration the degree of danger of a thing, as it could be very delicate to set out the criteria for assessing which things are more dangerous than others.

150. Second, there has to be causation[241] between the action of a thing (*fait de la chose*) and the harm (*dommage*).[242] If there was contact between the seat of harm and a thing in movement, there is a presumption that the thing is the legal cause of the harm caused to a third party. The only way to exonerate the guardian is to prove the existence of force majeure. If there was no contact between the thing and the seat of harm, there will be causation between the action of that thing and the seat of harm only if there was an abnormality as to the composition or the position of the thing at the moment when the harm was caused. This interpretation, taken from French case law, was applied in the cases *Mauritius Union Assurance v. Municipal Council of Beau-Bassin-Rose Hill* of 2011[243] and *Gunnoo Robin v. Mahatma Gandhi Institute* of 2006, dealt with by the Intermediate Court.[244] In the first case, a car was damaged when it passed over a metallic protection on a public road under which a hole was created in the course of public works. The metallic protection was supposed to withstand the pressure of the vehicle, but it did not and the car fell into the hole and was damaged. The Court considered that there had been contact between the thing that was not moving (the metallic protection) and the seat of harm (the damaged car) and that there was causation as there was the abnormality in the structure of the thing: the metallic protection was supposed to resist the weight of the vehicle, but there was an internal defect in it and the metallic protection did not resist the weight of the vehicle. In the second case, an individual fell and got hurt while he was using the stairs. The Court was of the view that in spite of the fact that the contact took place between the thing that was not moving and the seat of harm,

240. *See*, under French law, Rémy Cabrillac, *Droit des obligations* (Dalloz, 14th ed. 2020) paras 253–257.
241. Cabrillac, *supra* n. 241, at paras 247–248 and 258–259.
242. The seat of harm (*siège du dommage*) is either the body of a victim or a material thing that has been destroyed or damaged.
243. 2011 INT 28.
244. 2006 INT 73.

the thing was the legal cause of the harm, as there was an abnormality in the composition of the thing (the stairs were not well levelled).

151. The abnormality test applies when there is no contact between the act of the thing and the seat of harm. If the position or the composition of the thing was not normal, it would be considered the legal cause of the harm, even though there was no contact between it and the seat of harm.

152. Third, the person who is liable for the harm caused by a thing is its guardian.[245] This is provided by Article 1385(5) Civil Code. However, this paragraph does not give a definition of the guardian. We are of the view that the guardian may be defined as the person who has the independent power, whether this power is legal or illegal, to use, direct and monitor the thing.

153. Very often, the guardian of the thing is its owner, as this is the person vested by the law[246] with the power to use, direct and monitor it. In the case *Mohamed & Anor v. Virginie & Anor* of 2010, the Intermediate Court held that the owner has been confirmed as the guardian of the thing.[247]

154. Agents (*préposés*) who are simply carrying out the orders of their principal (*commettant*), their employer, for instance, do not qualify as guardians because they do not hold the independent power to use, direct and monitor the thing. They can be liable in tort for their civil fault but not as guardians of a thing under Article 1384(5) Civil Code. This is clearly set out in the cases *Appasawmy v. The Albatross Insurance Co* of 1997,[248] *Sun Insurance Co Ltd v. Government of Mauritius* of 1992[249] and *General Leasing Co Ltd & Anor v. State of Mauritius* of 2008.[250]

155. Thieves can also be considered guardians and liable under Article 1384(5) Civil Code, as they have the independent, although illegal, power to use, direct and monitor the thing. This stems from the cases *Appasawmy v. The Albatross Insurance Co* of 1997[251] and *Yip Tat Chung Sichi & Anor v. Cargo Handling Corporation & Anor* of 2006.[252]

156. A person to whom the owner has transferred the right to use, direct and monitor the thing may qualify as a guardian and be liable under Article 1384(5) Civil Code. For instance, if there is a contract transferring to another person the right to use a thing (e.g., a loan or a rental agreement), the user of the thing will be considered guardian of the thing under Article 1384(5) Civil Code. This interpretation has been confirmed by the Supreme Court. In the case *Mohulu v. Musruck* of

245. Cabrillac, *supra* n. 241, at paras 260–262.
246. Article 544 Civil Code, which gives the definition of property.
247. 2010 INT 240.
248. 1997 MR 98.
249. 1992 SCJ 85.
250. 2008 INT 375.
251. 1997 MR 98.
252. 2006 SCJ 127.

1996,[253] the Court held that, first of all, there had been a deposit contract between the owner of a car and the mechanic who was repairing that car. This contract has transferred to the mechanic the power to direct and monitor the vehicle. However, the mechanic was not held liable because, at the time when the harm was caused to the claimant, the vehicle had been used, directed and monitored by one of the mechanic's apprentices, who took possession of the vehicle without the consent of his principle (the mechanic). In the case *Chetty v. Gaindoo & Ors* of 2015,[254] the Supreme Court held that a father, who has been officially registered as the owner of a vehicle, has never been the guardian thereof, as the use, the direction and the monitoring of the vehicle have been transferred immediately after its purchase to his son, who became the guardian of the vehicle under Article 1384(5) Civil Code, and not the father.

157. The Civil Code is silent about the capacity of discernment of the guardian under Article 1384(5). For instance, can a five-year-old boy be considered the guardian of the stick that he had with him and with which he hurt another child? To our best knowledge, the Supreme Court has not yet answered this question. We are of the view that infants may also qualify as guardians under Article 1384(5) Civil Code, as they have the factual power to use, direct and monitor things which are in their hands. They do not need to possess the capacity of discernment. This is perfectly in line with the objective (strict) nature of the liability of a guardian under Article 1384(5) Civil Code: what matters is the risk that is under the guardian's control and not his or her ability to understand and regret the harmful consequence suffered by a third party.

§2. Exoneration of the Guardian

158. According to Article 1384(6) Civil Code, only force majeure or an exclusive civil fault of the victim may exonerate the guardian. This means that guardians may not be exonerated if they prove that they did not commit a civil fault (i.e., they have acted as they should have under the given circumstances) or that the harm is due to an internal defect of the thing under his or her control and direction. This has been confirmed in the case *General Construction Co Ltd v. Ibrahim Cassam & Co Ltd* of 2011.[255]

159. Force majeure is a natural event or a human action[256] external to the action of the thing, reasonably unforeseeable,[257] and reasonably irresistible as to its consequences.

253. 1996 SCJ 306.
254. 2015 SCJ 366.
255. 2011 SCJ 19.
256. In French, it is called *fait d'un tiers*. *See Fernandes v. Sawmynaden & Ors* [2020 SCJ 169].
257. *Fatehmamode & Co Ltd v. United Docs* [1979 SCJ 430]; *General Construction Co Ltd v. Ibrahim Cassam & Co Ltd* [2011 SCJ 19].

160. An exclusive fault of the victim is very similar to force majeure as it needs to be reasonably unforeseeable and its consequences have to be reasonably irresistible. It has to be noted that since the case *Medine Sugar Estates Co Ltd v. Anthony* of 1990,[258] a claimant can commit a civil fault even when he or she does not possess the capacity of discernment. In that case, a minor victim who did not possess the capacity of discernment entered the tiger's cage and was seriously wounded. In spite of the absence of the victim's capacity of discernment, the Supreme Court considered that the claimant had committed a civil fault as he did not behave as a prudent and reasonable person should have behaved under the same circumstances. The Supreme Court also was of the view that the fault of the minor victim was the exclusive reason for the suffered harm, although the fence separating the tiger from the public was a very low one (a height of around 75 cm). One may wonder whether the harmful consequence has been reasonably inevitable in those circumstances and whether the victim's fault was the exclusive cause of his harm. The total exoneration of the guardian has also been confirmed in the cases *Veeren v. State Insurance Company of Mauritius (Sicom) Ltd* of 2019[259] and *Toorab v. La Prudence Mauricienne Assurance Co Ltd* of 2016.[260] Thus, if an elderly lady suddenly changes the direction of her movement, steps on the road and is killed by a vehicle, the owner of the vehicle who was driving it will not be liable under Article 1384(5) Civil Code, as the action of the lady has been reasonably unforeseeable and the harmful consequence has been reasonable inevitable.

161. In case the victim commits a civil fault that has not been reasonably unforeseeable and inevitable from the guardian's point of view, the latter will be partially exonerated from his or her liability in tort. This was clearly set out in the case of *Rose Belle SE Board v. Chateauneuf Ltd* of 1990.[261] However, it is noteworthy that in 2021, in the case *Phoenix Insurance,* the Court adhered to a strict interpretation of Article 1384(6) Civil Code: the contributory negligence committed by the victim is not taken into account and cannot partially exonerate the guardian of the thing.[262]

§3. Special Regimes of Liability in Tort for Things

162. According to Article 1385 of the Mauritian Civil Code, the owner of an animal, or a person using it, is liable for the harm caused by that animal to third parties, even though at the moment when the harm was caused, the animal was not in the hands of its owner or its user and has escaped or lost itself.

163. Article 1385 is applicable to all animals as long as the animal has a master, i.e., someone who uses it, directs it and monitors it. However, in case the harm was caused by a wild animal without a master, such as a swarm of savage bees, Article

258. 1990 SCJ 334. *See also Appasawmy v. The Albatross Insurance Co* [1997 SCJ 180].
259. 2019 SCJ 267.
260. 2016 SCJ 370.
261. 1990 MR 9 and 16.
262. 2021 SCJ 364.

1385 Civil Code will not apply. This was clearly confirmed in the case *Nundloll v. Fuel* of 1992.[263] When a wild animal has a master, for instance, in a circus, Article 1385 is applicable to the owner of that wild animal.

164. Article 1385 is applicable to the guardian of the animal, i.e., to the owner or the person who uses, directs and controls the animal at the moment when the harm is caused. The liability of the guardian is a strict one, and the only way to escape liability in tort is to prove a force majeure or an exclusive fault of a victim. However, the guardian of the animal cannot be exonerated from his or her liability by proving that he or she did not commit any civil fault, for instance, that the animal has escaped due to an internal default of the cage in which it was locked.

165. According to Article 1386 Civil Code, the owner of a building is liable for all the harm that is caused by the total or partial destruction of the building when the destruction is due to a lack of maintenance or a vice of construction.

263. 1992 SCJ 383.

Chapter 2. Road and Traffic Accidents

166. Unlike in numerous other jurisdictions, the law of Mauritius does not provide for a liability regime specific to road and traffic accidents. Claimants have no choice but to invoke the general provisions of civil liability. In many cases, claimants and defendants will have no contractual relationship so that the compensation claim can only be based on fault (Articles 1382–1383 Civil Code) or on the liability for things under Article 1384(5) Civil Code. In these situations, the state of the law corresponds more or less to the tort law in France that was in effect prior to the enactment of a particularly strict liability regime under the *loi Badinter* in 1985.[264] In cases where the claimant and the defendant are parties to a contract, e.g., a contract of carriage, the *non-cumul* rule, already mentioned,[265] will operate, leaving the claimant with no option as to the legal cause of action: the compensation claim will have to be brought in contract on the grounds that the carrier has not complied with the 'safety obligation' (*obligation de sécurité*).[266]

167. In a non-contractual context, the 1983 legislative reform, which inserted in Article 1384 a new paragraph providing for a legal basis of the liability regime for harm caused by things,[267] led to a debate on the appropriate cause of action for traffic accident compensation. In *Mauritius Rose Belle S.E. Board v. Chateauneuf Ltd.*, the Supreme Court held that, in the light of the 1983 Act, there is 'no doubt whatsoever that the Mauritian Courts must in cases of road accidents involving motor vehicles now apply the provisions of (paragraphs) 1, 5 and 6 of Art. 1384'.[268] There is a widespread belief among Mauritian tort lawyers that fault-based liability under Article 1382 no longer corresponds with the main function of civil responsibility in the field of traffic accident compensation.[269] However, in a 1991 case, the Supreme Cort decided that the fault-based liability is still a valid ground for action and that, unlike the provisions of the French *loi Badinter*, Article 1384 is not an exclusive legal basis for a compensation claim.[270] It is not uncommon in Mauritian legal practice that a claim is brought on the basis of both Articles 1382–1383 and 1384 Civil Code.[271]

168. The application of the fault-based liability under Articles 1382–1383 Civil Code does not call for any particular comments. The legal appreciation of the defendant's conduct will often be based on the question of whether the car driver complied with the provisions of the Road Traffic Act at the time of the accident.

---

264. On the specific features of this liability regime, *see* e.g., Knetsch, *supra* n. 59, at paras 174–180 (with numerous references in the English language). For an overview of the pre-1985 situation in France, *see* Henri Mazeaud, Léon Mazeaud, Jean Mazeaud & André Tunc, *Traité théorique et pratique de la responsabilité civile délictuelle et contractuelle*, vol. 3/2 (Montchrestien, 6th ed. 1970) paras 1259–1263.
265. *See* paras 57–59 above.
266. For more details, *see* below para. 177.
267. *See* para. 149 above.
268. *Mauritius Rose Belle SE Board v. Chateauneuf Ltd* [1990 SCJ 30].
269. *See*, for example, Nuvin Proag, *An Appraisal of our Law of Torts in the Field of Road Accidents* (thesis Mauritius, 1991) 4.
270. *V Mohun v. Sunassee* [1991 SCJ 79].
271. *See*, for example, *Gopall & Ors v. Gannoo & Anor* [2023 SCJ 80].

Exceeding applicable speed limits,[272] using a phone whilst driving,[273] leaving a vehicle in a dangerous position,[274] etc., will be held as *faute* against the defendant. The choice of the liability for *faute* is, however, a double-edged sword, as the defendant may invoke the claimant's contributory negligence very easily, as the legislation does not provide for any restriction to the defendant's exoneration, contrary to what is laid down in Article 1384 for the liability for things.[275]

169. It is indeed much more beneficial for the claimant to invoke strict liability for the action of things provided for in Article 1384(5) Civil Code and already presented in the previous chapter.[276] Suffice it here to note that the conditions for this liability regime to be met are the action of a thing (*fait d'une chose*),[277] the damage and the causal link between the action of a thing and the damage. When those conditions are fulfilled, the proof of a blameworthy behaviour of the defendant is explicitly not required. The defendant will be liable on the sole ground that he or she is the guardian (*gardien*) of the vehicle, i.e., the vehicle's owner or the person who, at the time of the accident, had the power to use, direct and monitor it. Another major difference with the fault-based liability under Article 1382–1383 Civil Code is related to contributory negligence. As already mentioned, according to Article 1384(6) Civil Code, the claimant's fault does not always have an effect on entitlement to damages. Contrary to what is provided for in the general rules of civil liability, the defendant can only raise the argument that the accident has been caused by the 'exclusive fault' of the victim.[278] As for the force majeure defence, also mentioned in Article 1384(6) Civil Code, it refers to a natural event or a human action, provided that it is external to the thing, reasonably unforeseeable, and reasonably irresistible as to the consequences of the event, as laid out in the case law on general tort law.[279]

170. Even though the law of Mauritius applicable to traffic accidents departs significantly from the French law, it is not unusual that the Supreme Court refers to the *loi Badinter*, especially when it comes to delineating the contributory negligence defence available to the guardians of the vehicle and their insurer. For example, in a case of 2022, the Supreme Court reminded that 'unlike what obtains in France, since Article 1384 alinéas 1, 5 and 6 of the Civil Code in Mauritius do not provide that the *faute* of the victim can lead to partial exoneration of the *gardien* from liability, as a result, there cannot be any contributory negligence on the part of a victim

272. Section 124 Road Traffic Act.
273. Section 123T Road Traffic Act.
274. Section 123AE Road Traffic Act.
275. *See* para. 161 above.
276. *See* paras 149–164 above.
277. In most cases, the claimant will not have to establish an abnormality of the vehicle to proof the 'action of a thing'. As already mentioned (*see* para. 153 above), if there is a contact between the 'seat' of the harm (e.g., the claimant or property damaged) and a vehicle in movement, it will be presumed that the vehicle is the legal cause of the damage.
278. *See* recently *Phoenix Insurance (Mauritius) Ltd v. Mauritius Union Assurance Co Ltd & Anor* [2021 SCJ 364]; *Rosalie & Anor v. Sun Insurance Co Ltd* [2022 SCJ 147].
279. *See* para. 161 above.

of a road accident'.[280] In another case, the judges held that 'French case-law on Article 3 of the *loi Badinter* is of no assistance to our Courts, that the threshold to be reached under our law is much lower and that it is enough for the defendant at the trial to prove that the accident has been caused by the *faute exclusive* of the victim, irrespective of the gravity of the *faute.*'[281]

171. A less-explored issue in the tort law of Mauritius is the liability regime that applies to traffic accidents involving passengers bound by a contract with a carrier, such as a bus or a taxi company. Since the inauguration of a light rail transport system between Port Louis and Curepipe, the same question has arisen with regard to an accident affecting passengers of the *Metro Express*.[282] The case law of Mauritius does not seem reluctant to a liability in contract and not in tort on the basis of the violation of a so-called *obligation de sécurité*, i.e., the obligation to convey the passengers safely and sound to their destination.[283]

172. Regardless of the contractual or extra-contractual nature of the guardian of the vehicle, it should be noted that it is in the claimants' interest to enforce their right to compensation not against the tortfeasor but against his or her insurance company. Article 55 of the Road Traffic Act provides for a compulsory third-party insurance for the use of motor vehicles, and Article 1983-60 Civil Code entitles the injured party to a direct action (*action directe*) against the insurer.[284] In most cases, claims arising from road accidents will thus be settled by an insurance company; in so-called hit-and-run cases, the injured party may claim compensation from the Insurance Industry Compensation Fund, set up in 2005 and financed by the insurance companies according to Articles 88–89 of the Insurance Act. However, a governmental regulation makes clear that a payment made by this fund 'shall not exceed 350,000 rupees',[285] which may be regarded as insufficient in cases of serious bodily injury.

173. While the compulsory third-party insurance corresponds to international standards, the lack of a specific liability regime for road traffic accidents is subject to criticism. The Law Reform Commission of Mauritius repeatedly suggested the enactment of civil liability rules designed to improve the legal position of accident victims. In a 2017 Issue Paper, the Commission recommended adding a series of

---

280. *Phoenix Insurance (Mauritius) Ltd v. Mauritius Union Assurance Co Ltd & Anor* [2021 SCJ 364].
281. *Toorab v. La Prudence Mauricienne Assurance Co Ltd* [2016 SCJ 370].
282. The Light Rail Act of 2019 does not mention the applicable civil liability regime. However, according to Articles 15–19 of this Act, the operator of the light rail has to subscribe third party insurance.
283. *See* in particular *Dwarika & Anor v. Moka-Flacq Transport Ltd* [1973 MR 113]; *Butan v. The Rivière du Rempart Bus Service & Co Ltd* [1972 SCJ 189] ('It is now settled law that a carrier, who is bound under his contract to convey his passenger safe and sound to his destination (…).').
284. According to this provision, '(d)ans les assurances de responsabilité, les tiers lésés peuvent agir directement contre l'assureur, à la suite du fait dommageable'. On the functioning of this type of insurance, *see* Pravind Jugnauth, *Les principales réformes apportées aux assurances de dommages en droit mauricien*, Mauritius Law Review 1988, 76–130; Andre Robert, *Brief overview of the law of insurance in Mauritius*, Mauritius Business Law Review 2010, No. 2, 14–19.
285. Article 19(3) Insurance (Industry Compensation Fund) Regulations of 2005.

provisions, based on the French *loi Badinter* and the French *Code des assurances*, to the Civil Code in order to accelerate the compensation procedure, frequently delayed by insurers who invoke the claimant's contributory fault or even force majeure.[286] However, for now, there seems to be no political support for a reform of this legal framework.

286. *See* Law Reform Commission, *Issue Paper 'Indemnisation des victimes d'accidents de la circulation & Réforme du Droit des Assurances'* (Law Reform Commission, 2017). *See* already Law Reform Commission, *Issue Paper 'Law of Contracts and Obligations under Code Civil Mauricien'* (Law Reform Commission, 2013) 214 ('Faut-il introduire dans notre Code civil le régime d'indemnisation des victimes d'accidents de la circulation?').

Chapter 3. Product Liability

174. As for road and traffic accidents, there is no specific liability regime in the tort law of Mauritius for damage caused by defective products.[287] Unlike in France, the Civil Code of Mauritius does not provide for a set of rules dedicated to the civil liability of their manufacturers and their distributors.[288] What corresponds in other jurisdictions to product liability is the application of the common rules of liability to cases in which an unsafe product caused harm to a person or property. According to the circumstances of the case, liability for products takes the form of contractual or extra-contractual liability.

175. Where there is no contractual link between the claimant and the defendant, the civil liability of the manufacturer is mainly based on fault (Articles 1382–1383 Civil Code) or on Article 1384 (1) and (6) Civil Code, i.e., the liability for the action of things (*responsabilité du fait des choses*). The establishment of a fault is facilitated by section 3(1) of the Consumer Protection Act, according to which '(n)o person shall supply or import any goods which suffer from any fault with regard to any proscribed quality, quantity, potency, purity or standard or, in the case of any machinery or motor vehicle, with regard to the quality, nature or manner of its performance'. In other words, the marketing and importation of defective products is considered an infringement of a standard of conduct set out by the law.[289] However, it has to be said that the case law in this field is scarce, and the Supreme Court of Mauritius has not yet taken any judgment on the criteria that should lead trial judges to determine *fault* in product liability cases. Despite extensive research, we could not find any case in which the Supreme Court judges referred to product liability rules applicable in Europe.

176. According to the *non-cumul* rule,[290] the liability for damage caused by a defective product will be based on contract, if the claimant and the defendant were bound by a contractual relation, e.g., a sales contract (*contrat de vente*), regulated in Articles 1582–1701 Civil Code. In this case, the seller will be liable on the grounds of a *vice caché*, i.e., a 'hidden defect', triggering the seller's warranty (*garantie*) in accordance with Article 1641 Civil Code. It is important to note that under Article 1642 Civil Code, buyers have to prove that they have been reasonably careful when receiving the product, as the seller is not liable for *vices apparents*, i.e., 'visible defects'. However, one has to bear in mind that, under French law, professional sellers (*vendeurs professionnels*) are deemed to know about 'visible defects' and, therefore, precluded from raising the defence of the defect's visibility. It is still unclear whether this interpretation of Article 1642 is also implemented in the law of Mauritius.[291]

---

287. *See* Ariranga G Pillay, *Product Liability in Mauritius*, Mauritius Law Review 1977, No. 1, 45–58.
288. Law Reform Commission, *Issue Paper 'Law of Contracts and Obligations under Code Civil Mauricien'*, *supra* n. 287, at 215 ('notre Code civil ne contient pas de dispositions sur la responsabilité du fait du produit défectueux').
289. *Donald & Anor v. King Bros Co Ltd & Anor* [2022 SCJ 143]. For another application *see Iyemparooma v. CIP Ltée* [2010 INT 178].
290. *See* paras 54–64 above.
291. Pillay, *supra* n. 288, at 56–57 (the author refers to French case law).

177. Although the lack of a specific product liability regime has been noted by the Law Reform Commission in a 2013 issue paper,[292] there are no indications for current reform plans in this field of tort law.

292. Law Reform Commission, *Issue Paper 'Law of Contracts and Obligations under Code Civil Mauricien'*, *supra* n. 287, at 215.

Chapter 4. Liability for Service

178. The tort law of Mauritius does not provide for any strict liability regime for services. A service provider is subject to the general provisions of contractual liability as well as the specific liability rules governing each type of contract. According to the *non-cumul* principle,[293] a compensation claim can be made on an extra-contractual basis, for example, under fault (Articles 1382–1383 Civil Code), only in those cases in which there is no contractual relationship between the claimant and the defendant.

293. *See* paras 54–64 above.

Chapter 5. Environmental Liability

179. Over the last decades, the protection of the environment has become a matter of concern both for the Mauritian society and the legal community. Though incomplete, the regulation enacted by Parliament and Government today constitutes a singular branch of law, giving rise to a significant body of academic literature.[294] However, despite the increasing awareness among Mauritian lawyers and politicians for the importance of legal instruments in climate protection,[295] the assessment of liability issues related to environmental law is still at its beginnings and has more to do with prospective analysis than with the current state of law.[296]

180. Traditionally, the general tort law rules play an important role in environmental litigation, where ecological harm is accompanied by individual loss of health or property. In those cases, claimants can bring a civil action before the courts on the grounds of liability for fault (Articles 1382–1383 Civil Code) or for the action of things (Article 1384(1) and (6) Civil Code). In the particular field of environmental litigation, claimants often seek remedies on the basis of private nuisance (*troubles anormaux de voisinage*), which has long been seen as a restriction on property rights rather than as a liability regime.[297] In the law of Mauritius, a fault can result from non-compliance with environmental regulations, such as the standards enacted to ensure air quality, to limit soil pollution or to prevent the disposal of hazardous substances, etc.[298] Regardless of any precise environmental regulation, the Supreme Court also held that the operation of an industrial site can amount to *faute* if the operating conditions do not prevent air pollution sufficiently and cause bodily injury to one of the residents in the neighbourhood.[299]

---

294. *See* in particular Odile Lim Tung, *Environmental Law in Mauritius* (Kluwer Law International, 2nd ed. 2022); *Development and Balancing of Interests in Environmental Policy and Law in Mauritius*, in *The Balancing of Interests in Environmental Law in Africa* (Michael Faure & Willemien Du Plessis eds., Pretoria University Law Press 2012) 261–294; *Rethinking Environment Impact Assessment and Precaution in Mauritius* 61 (2017) Journal of African Law 227–251; *Quelques réflexions sur l'environnement et la Constitution mauricienne*, in *The 50th Anniversary of Mauritius. Constitutional Development* (Jacques Colom, Stephanie Rohlfing-Dijoux & Götz Schulze eds., Nomos 2019) 113–133; *Justice climatique, énergie et environnement : quelles perspectives contre l'inaction climatique à Maurice?* Revue juridique de l'océan Indien 2021, No. 31, 273–292; Pierre de Boucherville Baissac, *Mauritius*, in *South African Environmental Legislation Handbook* (Bryony Walmsley & Saphira Patel eds., South African Institute for Environmental Assessment 2012) 109–124; Rajendra Gunputh, *Développement durable et changements climatiques dans les petits États insulaires en développement: quelles responsabilités législatives et constitutionnelles à l'île Maurice?* Revue juridique de l'océan Indien 2021, No. 31, 205–226.
295. *See*, for example, section 2 of the Environment Protection Act ('It is declared that every person in Mauritius shall use his best endeavours to preserve and enhance the quality of life by caring responsibly for the natural environment of Mauritius.').
296. *See* however Lim Tung, *Environmental Law in Mauritius*, *supra* n. 295, at 317–326; Goran Georgijevic, *L'entrepreneuriat, le développement durable et la responsabilité délictuelle – Droit mauricien*, Revue juridique de l'environnement 2013, 433–447.
297. *See* paras 187–192 below. For examples specific to environmental pollution, *see* Lim Tung, *Environmental Law in Mauritius*, *supra* n. 295, at 325.
298. For detailed examples, *see* Georgijevic, *supra* n. 297, at 439–440.
299. *Dubillon & Ors v. Hervet* [2007 SCJ 188].

181. The Environment Protection Act 2002[300] refers to the common rules of civil liability, providing in section 23 that 'Article 1384 alinéa 1 of the Code Napoleon shall apply to an action' that is brought to court by 'any person affected in any way by a spill'.[301] This provision also states that 'the owner of a pollutant which is spilled shall always be deemed to be the "*gardien*" of the pollutant' and that 'a pollutant shall always be deemed to be in the custody of the owner of the pollutant', suggesting that the owner of the pollutant is not eligible to a rebuttal of the presumption of guardianship, as set out in the case law related to Article 1384(1) Civil Code.[302]

182. The liability of public authorities, subject to the proof of gross administrative misconduct (*faute lourde de l'administration*),[303] may also be considered, even though there is very limited case law in this field. In a case of 2002, the Supreme Court acknowledged the civil liability of the Central Electricity Board, a parastatal body owned by the State, in a case in which the operation of a power station in Port Louis caused a level of noise, vibration and pollution that constituted a health hazard to the claimants.[304] However, it is worth mentioning that section 93 Environment Protection Act 2002 puts a limitation to an action for damages against the Minister in charge of environmental affairs, the Director of Environment, the Island Chief Executive of Rodrigues and the *Police de l'Environnement* for any act 'done in good faith' in the execution of their powers under this Act.

183. The situation is more complicated in cases in which the harm invoked is to the environment itself, also known as *préjudice écologique pur* under French law. The main difficulty with these tort law claims is that for a claim to be granted in tort, the claimant has to establish a 'personal loss' (*dommage personnel*), which explains why the Mauritian courts are very reluctant to award legal redress for ecological harm. While the Supreme Court raised the issue of *préjudice écologigue* in a case of 2010,[305] there is no reliable legal basis in the law of Mauritius for the compensation of 'pure environmental harm'. The Parliament and the Government do not seem to consider the enactment of an act similar to the French 2016 Act on Biodiversity, which implemented in the Civil Code an action 'to repair ecological

300. *See* already s. 27 of the Environment Protection Act 1991. On this text, *see* Etienne Sinatambou, *The Approach of Mixed Legal Systems: The Case of Mauritius*, in *Environmental Damage in International and Comparative Law: Problems of Definition and Valuation* (Michael Bowman & Alan Boyle eds, OUP 2002) 270–279.
301. On this text, *see* Lim Tung, *Environmental Law in Mauritius*, *supra* n. 295, at 325–326; Georgijevic, *supra* n. 297, at 440–441.
302. *See* paras 155–159 above.
303. The most blatant example is probably the 2004 *Conseil d'État* judgment in which the French state was ordered to pay damages to asbestos victims for having banned asbestos usage too late (CE, 3 Mar. 2004, No. 241150). For a more detailed presentation, *see* Geneviève Viney, Patrice Jourdain & Suzanne Carval, *Les régimes spéciaux et l'assurance de responsabilité* (LGDJ, 4th ed. 2017) at para. 196, n. 20.
304. *Toofaneeram & Ors v. The Central Electricity Board* [2002 SCJ 216].
305. *Mohaiyuddin & Ors v. Emtel Limited* [2010 SCJ 425].

harm'.[306] In the legal literature, it is argued that public enforcement of environmental regulation could be more efficient than private compensation claims.[307] It should be noted, however, that section 32(5) of the Environment Protection Act 2002 provides that '(i)f the damage caused by the spill, affects the environment or any property, object or thing which is not privately owned, the Attorney-General may claim damages against the owner of the pollutant', addressing cases, in which the spill affects land in public ownership.

184. Lastly, Mauritian courts are also reluctant to give legal effect to the so-called precautionary principle (*principe de précaution*), which was enshrined in the French constitution in 2004. According to this principle, even in the absence of conclusive scientific knowledge or evidence that a given activity is harmful or dangerous to human health, it is sufficient that such a risk exists for the operation of such an activity to be immediately prohibited. It is argued that, applied to actions in tort, this principle could give rise to a preventive form of civil liability.[308] In a case of 2010, in which the claimant asked for an interlocutory injunction to stop a mobile phone company from operating a cell phone antenna, the Supreme Court mentioned this principle but decided to set it aside on the grounds that '(i)t has not been established (…) that there is any such risk to the health of the applicants either in the short or long term, which may be caused by the emission of the electromagnetic radiation and which would justify the issue of an interlocutory injunction'.[309]

306. On the current situation under French law, *see* Knetsch, *supra* n. 59, at paras 191–193.
307. Georgijevic, *supra* n. 297, at 442–444.
308. For the Mauritian legal literature, *see* Georgijevic, *supra* n. 297, at 444–446.
309. *Mohaiyuddin & Ors v. Emtel Limited* [2010 SCJ 425].

Chapter 6. Private Nuisance (*troubles anormaux de voisinage*)

185. As in other jurisdictions, the remedy for disturbances between neighbours is based on the idea that in the enjoyment of their premises, individuals must ensure not to interfere excessively with their neighbours. In the tort law of Mauritius, neither one of the liability regimes mentioned above has proven appropriate to provide a satisfactory legal basis for the redress for such kind of property infringement. Consequently, the Supreme Court decided, once again, to use the French case law to build a doctrine of *troubles anormaux de voisinage*.

186. The French Court of Cassation erected a proper regime for nuisance as an autonomous ground of civil liability,[310] progressively abandoning the reference to the doctrine of *faute* under Article 1382 Civil Code. According to a landmark decision in 1844,[311] a claimant does not have to establish fault but only a *trouble anormal de voisinage*, that is, a serious disturbance exceeding the normal inconvenience or discomfort between neighbours. This departure from the *faute* doctrine means that an owner or a tenant can be held liable even though every measure of precaution was taken which a prudent individual, anxious not to disturb his neighbours, would have taken. The idea of civil liability without fault was adopted by the Supreme Court in a case of 1981[312] and has been reiterated ever since.[313]

187. For the purposes of the doctrine of *troubles anormaux de voisinage*, the term *voisinage* is not to be taken too literally. The regime is not limited to immediate neighbours but applies to all those living in the same 'neighbourhood' (*communauté de voisinage*), regardless of their legal status. An owner will thus be treated on an equal footing with a tenant or a beneficiary of any other right to use land or a building. According to case law, it is irrelevant whether the claimant is actually the occupier of the land or the building, as long as it can be demonstrated that the disturbance resulted in a loss.[314]

188. Given the great variety of disturbances,[315] it is impossible to summarise the case law of the lower courts and to draw a line between *troubles* which must be endured by neighbours and those which exceed the *anormalité* threshold. To quote the Supreme Court, '(i)n cases where a *trouble de voisinage* is complained of, a

310. *See,* e.g., Civ 3, 19 Mar. 2020, No. 18-26360 ('vu le principe selon lequel nul ne doit causer à autrui un trouble anormal de voisinage').
311. *See* Civ, 27 Nov. 1844, Sirey 1844, 1, 211. *See also* Req, 20 Feb. 1849, D 1849, 1, 148.
312. *Ramgutty and Co Ltd v. Hanumanthadu* [1981 SCJ 321]. *See* already *Hermic Ltd v. Compagnie des Magasins Populaires Limitée and Anor* [1981 SCJ 162].
313. *Boodhoo v. Prefumo* [1987 MR 191]; *Dorasamy Kauppamuthoo v. Chotay Carrimbaccus* [1995 MR 259]; *Sabeer Hossen Baukar v. Boyrun & Ors* [2002 SCJ 260]; *Aubroo & Ors v. Municipality of Vacoas* [2005 SCJ 260]; *Jebodh v. Basant Roi* [2008 SCJ 244]; *Mohaiyuddin & Ors v. Emtel Limited* [2010 SCJ 425].
314. Civ 2, 28 Jun. 1995, 93-12681 (the owner of a building destined to be leased claimed damages on the ground that the disturbance caused a decrease in its rental value).
315. Noise, vibrations, smoke, smell, water pollution, unattractiveness of a building, shadowing, obstruction of views … .

defendant can only escape liability if he shows that he was not causing his neighbour a degree of abnormal inconvenience'.[316] For this purpose, judges take into account the properties of the neighbourhood, the frequency of the disturbances, their intensity, the existence of an easement (*servitude*) or other disturbances.[317] Unlike in France, where the Court of Cassation does not exercise a strict control on this test, the Supreme Court of Mauritius does not leave it to the lower courts to decide whether the circumstances warrant liability on this basis. In all the cases brought before the Supreme Court, the judges carefully reviewed both the consistency and the intensity of the *trouble* invoked to confirm or annul the redress awarded by the trial courts.

189. Where a *trouble anormal* is characterised, the judge can award damages to compensate for the impossibility of ceasing the disturbance or, as is more frequent, make an order for an injunction, interlocutory or permanent.[318] The situation is more complicated when the inconvenience arises from an installation which was approved by public authorities, for example, relay antennas for mobile phones or classified facilities. It turns out that in most cases brought before the Mauritian courts, the inconvenience resulted from an activity that was not covered by a permit, licence or authorisation. It is, therefore, uncertain whether a court would accept to issue an injunction or award damages, despite existing administrative authorizations. While it is settled case law in France that the mere existence of an administrative approval does not hinder neighbours from seeking redress before civil courts,[319] the legal situation in Mauritius seems more unclear.

190. Almost entirely case law-based,[320] the doctrine of *troubles anormaux de voisinage* has long been seen in the French legal doctrine as a part of property law, but it is now regarded by most legal scholars as an independent liability regime.[321] In the law of Mauritius, this connection to property law has never been as strong as under French law, as the Supreme Court pointed out in *Ramgutty*: '(w)hatever may be the correct theoretical basis, it is now well settled in France that "*l'exercice, même légitime, du droit de propriété devient générateur de responsabilité lorsque le trouble qui en résulte pour autrui dépasse la mesure des obligations ordinaires du voisinage*"'.[322]

---

316. *Boodhoo v. Prefumo* [1987 MR 191].
317. For a complete survey of criteria applied under French law, *see* e.g., Philippe le Tourneau (ed.), *Droit de la responsabilité et des contrats: Régimes d'indemnisation 2023–2024* (Dalloz, 13th ed. 2023) paras 2242.21–2242.22.
318. *See*, e.g., *Ah Fong Chan Yam Kwong & Anor v. Phil Alain Didier Co Ltd & Ors* [2013 SCJ 220].
319. On the interplay of administrative and civil law under French law, *see* Valérie Gaillot-Mercier, *Troubles de voisinage*, in *Répertoire de droit civil* (Dalloz, 2019) paras 16–17.
320. *See* in English, Ciara Kennefick, *Nuisance and Coming to the Nuisance. The Porous Boundary between Torts and Servitudes in England and France*, in *French Civil Liability in Comparative Perspective* (Jean-Sébastien Borghetti & Simon Whittaker eds, Hart 2019) 223.
321. However, the doctrine of *troubles anormaux de voisinage* does not exclusively apply. According to case law, claimants may choose to bring an action on the ground of *faute* if the occurrence of a *trouble anormal* can be regarded as a civil fault in the sense of Articles 1382–1383 Civil Code. *See*, e.g., *Ramnarain v. Dookhit* [2016 INT 460].
322. *Ramgutty and Co Ltd v. Hanumanthadu* [1981 SCJ 321].

Part IV. Defences and Exception Clauses

Chapter 1. Limitation of Action (*prescription extinctive*)

191. The rules governing the limitation of actions[323] are laid out in Articles 2268 to 2283 of the Civil Code of Mauritius. Unlike in France, where the legislature initiated a complete overhaul of the law of *prescription extinctive* in 2008, the situation in Mauritius is still similar to the rules enacted in the 1804 Code Napoléon, which dates back even further to the *Ancien Régime*. Since then, the rules governing the limitation of actions are laid out in Articles 2219 to 2254. Unlike in common law jurisdictions, 'extinctive prescription' not only concerns the procedural aspects of tort law but also refers to the substantive right to compensation. The predominant view in French legal literature is that of a hybrid nature: after expiry of the period of prescription, the debtor is entitled to refuse performance on the level of substantive law, but the relevant obligation is not entirely extinguished since a debtor who has paid in spite of prescription having occurred is unable to recover.

192. While there is no specific rule for compensation claims in tort, Article 2270 Civil Code provides for a general rule. According to this text, 'personal actions (*actions personnelles*) prescribe in ten years', this period running from the day 'the cause of action arises' (*jour où le droit d'action a pris naissance*).[324] In order to determine the starting point of the prescription period, the Mauritian courts frequently refer to the English case law and, in particular, to the definition of the legal term 'cause of action'. For example, in a judgment delivered in 2002, the Supreme Court held that '(t)he words "cause of action" comprise every fact (though not every piece of evidence) which it would be necessary for the plaintiff to prove, if traversed, to support his right to the judgment of the Court (*see Read v. Brown* (1888) 22 Q.B.D. 128 per Lord Esher M. R. p. 131)'.[325] While, on a theoretical level, this hybrid interpretation of the rules governing the limitation of action is remarkable, it is understandable when bearing in mind that the extinctive prescription under the

323. The choice of terminology in this field is rather unsatisfactory for a civil lawyer as the term 'limitation of actions' only refers to a procedural institution. 'Extinctive prescription' in the sense of Mauritian law also has substantive effects. *See* on this issue Reinhard Zimmermann, *'Extinctive' Prescription under the* Avant-projet, ERPL 2007, 805 (note 1) and by the same author, *Comparative Foundations of a European Law of Set-Off and Prescription* (CUP 2002) 21.

324. Article 2271 Civil Code.

325. *Bedacee v. Hookoomsing* [2002 SCJ 271]. *See also New Beau Bassin Cooperative Store v. Juggroo* [1980 MR 320] ('A "cause of action" is constituted by the averment of facts which, if denied, require to be proved to enable a Plaintiff to obtain the remedy he seeks.').

law of Mauritius is a genuinely hybrid institution, which borrows from substantive rules of the French Civil Code and procedural rules of Common Law origin.

193. In concrete terms, the prescription rule of Article 2270 Civil Code means that actions in tort or on the basis of contractual liability are subject to a ten-year period which begins to run from the day on which all the requirements for an action under tort are fulfilled, i.e., when a harm is caused by a tortious act (*fait générateur de responsabilité*), regardless of the occurrence of the initial harm's consequences.[326] In this respect, the law of Mauritius corresponds to the French law, as it applied prior to the 2008 reform of the rules governing the limitation of actions,[327] which means that in some cases, the starting point of the *délai de prescription* is postponed. For the purposes of tort law, the most important exception is the one set out in Article 2252 Civil Code, according to which the prescription period does not start running until a minor reaches the age of majority.[328] Contrary to what is set out in French law, there is no specific rule applicable to personal injury compensation claims, which means that, in Mauritius, *prescription extinctive* is running, even though the initial or aggravated injury is not stabilised yet. Thus, in cases in which the claimant invokes a progressive health condition due to a tortious act, the starting point of the ten-year-period will be the day of the first occurrence of the bodily harm so that the action in tort will be time-barred when claimants enter their case more than ten years after this date.

194. Following the example of the French law of *prescription extinctive*, the Mauritian law distinguishes between the suspension and the interruption of a prescription period. Whereas 'suspension' of the prescription temporarily stops its course without erasing the delay that has already run, 'interruption' erases the delay that has elapsed and causes a new period of the same duration as the former period to run. Suspension is governed by Articles 2251–2259 Civil Code, even though these provisions do not clearly separate the postponement of the starting point (*report du point de départ*) of a prescription period and its suspension *stricto sensu*. In the field of tort law, it is worth mentioning that prescription is suspended against adults under *tutelle* (Article 2252), between spouses (Article 2253) and, more generally, against individuals for whom it is impossible to bring an action before a court.[329] The latter cause of suspension is not explicitly mentioned in the Civil Code but has been acknowledged by the Supreme Court of Mauritius in several cases.[330] The courts are also tending to extend to the law of Mauritius causes of suspension, which are known only in common law. For example, in the case *Bundhoo v.*

326. For an example, *see Ramana Manchee Rajoo v. Saint Felix Sugar Estate Co Ltd* [2023 INT 27].
327. For an overview of the former rules of the French Civil Code, *see* Geneviève Viney & Patrice Jourdain, *Les effets de la responsabilité* (LGDJ, 2nd ed. 2001) para. 420.
328. For an application, *see* for example *Ferrat Marine v. Joseph Marie Michel de Ravel de Largentière* [2015 SCJ 225].
329. In the French-speaking legal literature, authors use the Latin phrase *contra non valentem agree non currit praescriptio* to express this idea.
330. *See*, for example, *National Cold Storage Co Ltd v. Lloyd's* [2007 SCJ 33]. *See* already *Receiver of Registration Dues v. Heirs of Lelia Aissa* [1910 MR 73]; *Suresh Chandrika Moorba v. Mrs Jean Francois Leslie Gaud* [1996 SCJ 341].

Bhugoo, the Supreme Court confirmed that it could stay a civil case for abuse of process and that a serious risk of not having a fair hearing can justify a delay in bringing a case.[331]

195. As for the interruption of the prescription period, the provisions laid out in Articles 2240–2250 Civil Code should be familiar to lawyers of other jurisdictions. The legislation recognises three major causes of interruption: the initiation of judicial proceedings, even by way of summary proceedings (*référé*); the acknowledgement of an obligation by its debtor (*reconnaissance de dette*); and an act of forced execution (*exécution forcée*). Among those causes, the initiation of judicial proceedings is undoubtedly the most important cause of interruption in tort litigation. The French Court of Cassation has decided that an action against the tortfeasor does not have any interruptive effect on the action against the tortfeasor's liability insurer.[332] To our knowledge, the Supreme Court of Mauritius has never addressed this issue, despite its practical importance.[333]

331. *Bundhoo v. Bhugoo & Anor* [1993 MR 243] [1995 MR 177]. *See also SICOM Ltd & Anor v. Soochet Devendra* [2007 INT 227].
332. Civ 2, 7 Feb. 2013, No. 12-12875.
333. On the specific prescription rules governing the action against an insurer, *see* Articles 1983-37–1983-38 Civil Code; *Daiboo v. La Prudence Mauricienne Assurances Ltd* [2018 SCJ 427].

Chapter 2. Grounds of Justification

196. Surprisingly, the Civil Code of Mauritius does not make any reference to defences such as consent (*consentement*), necessity (*état de nécessité*), self-defence (*légitime défense*) or legal duty/lawful authority (*ordre de la loi, permission de la loi, commandement de l'autorité légitime*). It was the responsibility of the Mauritian courts to develop a doctrine of *faits justificatifs* that limits the scope of fault-based liability, following the case law of both the French Court of Cassation and the English courts. Especially in the field of press and media litigation, the courts of Mauritius often refer to the *fait justificatif* of good faith,[334] unknown to the French law, introducing another example of hybridisation to the tort law of Mauritius. As the law of defamation is presented in another part of this monograph,[335] we will not go further into this issue. Furthermore, as some grounds of justification, such as the doctrine of abuse of rights (*abus de droit*) and contributory fault, are folded into the concept of fault and thus merged into the elements of liability,[336] we refer readers to other sections of this monograph as these concepts are more closely related to the definition of *fault* and to causation.[337]

197. Given the lack of explicit provisions in the Civil Code, the French doctrine of *faits justificatifs* has been elaborated on the basis of the Napoleonic Criminal Code of 1810, which recognised in Articles 327 to 329 that under certain circumstances, legal duty, lawful authority and self-defence defeat criminal liability. Those defences, as well as necessity (*état de nécessité*), are now enshrined in Articles 122-4 to 122-7 of the French Criminal Code. Generally speaking, it can be said that, like in other jurisdictions, the grounds of justification have received much greater academic attention in the field of criminal law than in tort law, so that tort lawyers in France tend, as a natural reflex, to refer to criminal law rather than to try to elaborate specific solutions.[338] However, there is agreement that in order to ensure the effectiveness of the primacy of criminal law over tort law (*le criminel tient le civil en l'état*), civil courts should follow as far as possible the solutions deriving from criminal law.

198. The situation in Mauritius is different. As already mentioned,[339] when it comes to the interplay of civil and criminal liability, the law of Mauritius follows the common law approach, which means that criminal and civil law are dealt with

334. *See* for example *Boodhoo v. Sun Printing Ltd* [1992 SCJ 208]; *Dookhony v. La Sentinelle Ltd & Anor* [2008 SCJ 61].

335. *See* para. 107 above.

336. For a recent comparative analysis, *see* Sandy Steel, *Defences to Tortious and Contractual Liability in French Law*, in *French Civil Liability in Comparative Perspective* (Jean-Sébastien Borghetti & Simon Whittaker eds, Hart 2019) 285, 288. *See also* Jean Limpens, Robert M Kruithof & Anne Meinertzhagen-Limpens, *Liability for One's Own Act*, in *International Encyclopedia of Comparative Law* vol. XI (André Tunc ed., Brill & J C B Mohr 1983) Ch. 2, paras 165–192.

337. *See* paras 101–104 above (doctrine of abuse of rights) and paras 206–209 below (contributory fault).

338. Steel, *Defences*, *supra* n. 337, at 295.

339. *See* paras 52–53 above.

as two separate issues and that there is no need for a strong congruency between both forms of liability.[340] It would be wrong, however, to presume that on the grounds of justification, the impact of French law on tort is inexistent. As will be shown hereafter, Mauritian courts often refer to the French case law and legal doctrine when addressing the issue of *faits justificatifs* and, thus, indirectly to the solutions prevailing in French criminal law. Nevertheless, there is only little case law emanating from the courts of Mauritius, which usually approach grounds of justification by listing them in the same way as textbooks in France.[341]

§1. CONSENT (*CONSENTEMENT DE LA VICTIME*)

199. Following the French law, the law of Mauritius provides that victim's consent is considered a justification under certain conditions so that the defendant's unlawful act may not be regarded as fault (*volenti non fit iniuria*).[342] When it comes to interferences with property (*atteinte à des biens matériels*) and personality rights, such as privacy (*droit à la vie privée*)[343] or sexual self-determination,[344] the victim's consent precludes liability and bars the compensation claim based on fault. In other cases, however, consent is deemed irrelevant as individuals cannot dispose of inalienable rights. In particular, apart from medical action,[345] interference with bodily integrity or life may not be excluded from the scope of civil liability on the sole ground that the claimant consented.

200. Closely related to the concept of consent, the doctrine of *acceptation des risques* ('acceptance of risk') has been referred to by the Supreme Court of Mauritius to raise the threshold of fault in cases in which personal injury was caused.[346]

---

340. Section 7(2) of the Criminal Procedure Act provides that '(t)he verdict or judgment in the one case shall not be admitted as evidence in the other'.
341. *See*, for example, *Boodhoo v. Sun Printing Ltd* [1992 SCJ 208] (quoting a French author, the judgment refers to 'les faits justificatifs de droit commun, la légitime défense, l'autorisation de la loi, l'état de nécessité').
342. In the field of tort law, it can be argued that consent is a general ground of justification and that this defence is excluded in specific cases. *See,* however, Limpens, Kruithof & Meinertzhagen-Limpens, *supra* n. 337, at para. 187 ('In French and Belgian law the consent of the victim does not remove the element of fault from the defendant's act.'). For a comparison of criminal and civil law, *see* Hajer Rouidi, *Une notion pénale à l'épreuve de la responsabilité civile: les faits justificatifs*, Revue de science criminelle et de droit pénal comparé 2016, 17.
343. In the law of press, the defendant may invoke the claimant's consent as a defence. However, according to the general provisions on proof in Art. 1315(2) Civil Code, it is up to the defendant to establish the claimant's consent to the interference (e.g., the publication of a photograph).
344. Likewise, there cannot be, in principle, any liability for rape, sexual harassment or *attentat à la pudeur* (ss 249 and 254 of the Criminal Code) if the defendant can establish the claimant's (full) consent, unless the claimant is a minor under the age of 16 or a mentally handicapped person (s. 249(4) of the Criminal Code).
345. *See*, for example, *Coonjah v. Soap and Allied Industries Ltd* [1977 MR 309].
346. *See*, on the French law, Geneviève Viney, Patrice Jourdain & Suzanne Carval, *Conditions de la responsabilité* (LGDJ, 4th ed. 2013) paras 573–573-1. In English, *see* Steel, *Defences*, *supra* n. 337, at 304.

According to the idea that the victim was aware of the risks when engaging in a dangerous activity, the Mauritian courts tend to adopt a more restrictive approach to fault-based civil liability.[347] However, following the solutions of the French law,[348] it was ruled that the doctrine of *acceptation des risques* could not be upheld against a claimant who based the claim on the general principle of liability for things (Article 1384(1) Civil Code).[349]

§2. Necessity (*État de nécessité*)

201. The idea that necessity (*état de nécessité*) excludes liability is not explicitly foreseen in the criminal law of Mauritius. The 1838 Criminal Code only provides for some scattered examples. For instance, section 235A provides for an authorisation of abortion in case 'the continued pregnancy will endanger the pregnant person's life' (2)(a) or if 'the termination is necessary to prevent grave permanent injury to the physical or mental health of the pregnant person' (b). What is more, the position of the Supreme Court of Mauritius in criminal cases is not entirely clear on this point. In several cases, the Court held that the defence of necessity should rather be understood as a defence of *contrainte* that can be invoked when 'the accused person (…) has been compelled to commit (a crime or misdemeanour) by a force which he could not resist', in accordance with section 42(1) of the Criminal Code.[350] It is, therefore, still unclear whether the French concept of *état de nécessité* can apply to the criminal law of Mauritius, even though the Supreme Court made it clear in the same cases that 'our law relating to excuses and defences that an accused may invoke at his trial (…) is governed by our Criminal Code' and that the relevant provisions 'are borrowed from the French Penal Code and we should seek guidance from the French Courts in interpreting them'.[351]

202. Due to the scarcity of case law, it is even more difficult to determine the civil consequences of an act of necessity or *contrainte* as defined by the criminal law.[352] Under French law, it is stated that an act of necessity in the sense of criminal law should exclude civil liability based on *faute* but should not leave the victim of

347. For an example in the context of a workplace accident, *see*, e.g., *Coonjah v. Soap and Allied Industries Ltd* [1977 MR 309].
348. Civ 2, 4 Nov. 2010, No. 09-65947.
349. *Seeraz v. Sooriah* [2010 SCJ 49].
350. *Seegobin v. The State* [2002 SCJ 163]; *State v. Dilmamode & Ors* [1995 MR 186].
351. *Seegobin v. The State* [2002 SCJ 163]; *State v. Dilmamode & Ors* [1995 MR 186].
352. According to the French law, there has to be 'a present or imminent danger to a person or property' and 'proportionality between the unlawful act and the danger'. The courts also ensure that the act of necessity was 'socially useful' (*utile socialement*), i.e., the preserved interest is more important than the interest sacrificed, and that the author of the act did not cause the state of necessity by his own fault. On those conditions, *see* Patrice Jourdain, *Responsabilité fondée sur la faute: Faits justificatifs*, in *JurisClasseur Civil Code*, Art. 1382 à 1386, fasc 121-20 (LexisNexis, 2012) paras 46–53.

this act without any form of compensation.[353] The situation in Mauritius is not entirely clear, as the Supreme Court has not yet had the opportunity to address this issue. Moreover, if the solutions adopted were to be the same as in France, there still would be a difficulty in determining the legal basis of the victim's right to compensation. Whereas some authors call for the enactment of a specific strict liability regime, others refer to the 'law of quasi-contracts' (*droit des quasi-contrats*) and, in particular, to unjust enrichment or *negotiorum gestio*.[354] Strikingly, in the few French cases in which necessity has been invoked before civil courts, the defence had been rejected on the grounds of the proportionality test or because an actual or imminent danger could not be characterised.[355]

§3. Lawful Defence (*Légitime Défense*)

203. Related to the doctrine of *état de nécessité*, the law of Mauritius also knows the concept of lawful defence (*légitime défense* or *défense légitime*) in order to exclude civil liability in cases in which the defendant acted in response to a threat against a person or property. Once again, the criminal law was the inspiration for this ground of justification as the Civil Code remains silent on *légitime défense*. According to section 246 of the 1838 Criminal Code, 'there is neither crime nor misdemeanor, where homicide, wounds or blows are commanded by an actual necessity of the lawful defence of oneself or another person'. If the requirements of self-defence are fulfilled (unjustified attack, actual or imminent; concurrent response, necessary and proportionate),[356] the courts will reject the claim for compensation based upon the civil liability for fault. While there is (little) case law on self-defence as a ground of justification in criminal law,[357] we have not been able to find any relevant judgment on the civil law dimension of *légitime défense*.

§4. Others

204. The Mauritian case law also refers to lawful authority (*permission de la loi*) and to an order emanating from a legitimate authority (*commandement de l'autorité légitime*) as defences which can be invoked in civil liability cases.[358] While there is no explicit case applying this ground of justification, the legislation of Mauritius provides examples of legal immunities awarded to specific groups of

353. *See*, e.g., Philippe Brun, *Responsabilité civile extracontractuelle* (LexisNexis, 6th ed. 2023) para. 346 (according to this author, a right of compensation should be granted 'in equity' [*équité*]). For an extensive survey, *see* Rouidi, *supra* n. 343, at paras 28–30.

354. Viney, Jourdain & Carval, *Conditions*, *supra* n. 347, at para. 571 (with further references). For a full survey, *see* Jourdain, *Responsabilité fondée sur la faute*, *supra* n. 353, at paras 54–62.

355. *See* the references in le Tourneau (ed.), *Droit de la responsabilité*, *supra* n. 318, at paras 2141.20–2141.24. *See also*, for an example of a Mauritian criminal case, *Seegobin v. The State* [2002 SCJ 163].

356. For an application of those criteria, *see*, e.g., *Police v. Pierre* [2008 INT 86].

357. *See* in particular *Teeluckdharry v. The Queen* [1957 MR 277].

358. *See*, for example, *Boodhoo v. Sun Printing Ltd* [1992 SCJ 208].

professionals: civil servants,[359] pleading lawyers[360] and elected officials[361] are regularly cited to illustrate the exonerating effect of lawful authority in the field of civil liability.[362] Civil law and criminal law often apply the same solution, with the legislation of Mauritius offering various examples explicitly excluding both civil and criminal liability.[363] In more general terms, section 245 of the Criminal Code provides that 'there is neither crime nor misdemeanour, where homicide, wounds or blows are ordered by law, and commanded by lawful authority'. Under French law, there is broad consensus that this rule should also apply in civil law, even though very little doctrinal attention has been given to this issue.[364] There is no reason why this solution should not extend to the law of Mauritius.

205. A closely related question is to what extent administrative permission (*autorisation administrative*) may exclude civil liability.[365] More and more economic activities are subject to prior approval by public authorities: the manufacture of pharmaceuticals or other potentially toxic products, the operation of industrial facilities, the installation of mobile phone towers, etc. According to the traditional standpoint of French law, the mere fact that public authorities have granted a permit does not exclude civil liability in case of negligence.[366] The reason is that public authorities cannot carry out all the verifications that are necessary to ensure the protection of everyone's interests. Moreover, the authorisation does not preclude the way the operator performs its activity, which explains why, in the field of environmental protection, administrative permission is granted 'subject to the rights of third parties' (*sous réserve des droits des tiers*).[367] To our knowledge, the Mauritian courts have not yet had the opportunity to address this issue.

359. *See* para. 101 above. *See also* section 93(1) of the Environment Protection Act, '(n)o civil or criminal liability shall attach to the Minister, the Director, the Island Chief Executive, the *Police de l'Environnement*, or to any authorised officer in respect of any act done in good faith in the execution or purported execution of their duties or their powers under this Act.' For more details on this provision, *see* para. 187 above.
360. According to Article 290 of the Criminal Code, pleading lawyers (barristers or advocates), the *Ministère Public* and witnesses cannot be judged for defamation (*diffamation*) or for slander (*injure*) with regard to declarations made before court. This privilege covers both criminal and civil liability.
361. Section 3 of the National Assembly (Privileges, Immunities and Powers) Act provides that '(n)o civil or criminal proceedings may be instituted against the Speaker or any member for words spoken before, or written in a report to, the Assembly or any committees (…)'.
362. One could also mention the immunity established in Article 258 of the Criminal Code. According to this provision, '(a)ny person who, without any order from the constitued authorities, and except in cases where the law directs the arrest of accused parties, detains, or sequesters any person, shall be punished (…)'.
363. Article 290 of the Criminal Code; section 3 of the National Assembly (Privileges, Immunities and Powers) Act; section 93(1) of the Environment Protection Act.
364. For a brief presentation, *see* Viney, Jourdain & Carval, *Conditions*, *supra* n. 347, at paras 562–562-1. *See also* in English Limpens, Kruithof & Meinertzhagen-Limpens, *supra* n. 337, at paras 181–182.
365. On this point, *see* Viney, Jourdain & Carval, *Conditions*, *supra* n. 347, at para. 561 and, in English, Limpens, Kruithof & Meinertzhagen-Limpens, *supra* n. 337, at para. 183.
366. *See,* e.g., in the field of liability for toxic products, Civ 2, 14 Jun. 1972, No. 71-11318 (the authorisation 'does not relieve those who accomplish the act from the duty of care [*obligation de prudence et de diligence*] under Article 1382 Civil Code').
367. Article L 514-19 Environmental Code (France).

Chapter 3. Contributory Fault

206. In Mauritius, where tort liability is defined as the obligation imposed by the law to compensate victims for all the losses they have suffered from an unlawful act, the main objective of the tort law is to place them in the position where they were before. This principle is known as the principle of full compensation (*principe de réparation intégrale*) and has been mentioned in the cases *Allymamod v. Nujjoo & Anor* of 2021 and *Cooppen & Anor v. New India Assurance Co Ltd* of 2022.[368] According to the first case, '(i)t is nevertheless still incumbent upon the plaintiff to prove each and every particulars of her claim in order to be fully compensated as the principle remains that of the *réparation intégrale*, that is neither a loss nor a profit'.[369]

207. However, a civil fault, defined as the behaviour that a reasonable and careful person would have had under the same circumstances, committed by the victim and not qualifying as force majeure may partly exonerate the tortfeasor. The extent of the exoneration will be directly proportionate to the gravity of the fault committed by the victim. For instance, if a court in Mauritius reaches the conclusion that the victim's fault has contributed to his or her loss by 40%, the amount of compensation granted to the victim will be reduced by 40%.

208. In the case *Coonjah v. Soap and Allied Industries Ltd* of 1977,[370] the Supreme Court held that the exoneration is proportionate to the gravity of the victim's fault. It has been established that the victim, a former employee of the defendant, had suffered body injury not only due to a fault committed by his former employer but also due to his own fault, as he was not wearing a health protection mask at his workplace. The court was of the view that the victim's fault had contributed 25% to his harm, and the compensation granted to the victim should thus been reduced by 25%. In the case *M & A Aluminium Centre Ltd v. The Mauritius Commercial Bank Ltd* of 2009,[371] the Supreme Court held that a client's fault had contributed by 50% to his harm and the liability of his bank was to be reduced to 50%.

209. The Mauritian courts adopted a similar stand point in the field of strict liability for things. In case a claimant commits a civil fault that has not been reasonably unforeseeable and inevitable from the guardian's point of view, the latter will be partly exonerated. This has been clearly set out in the case of *Rose Belle SE Board v. Chateauneuf Ltd* of 1990.[372] However, in the case of *Phoenix Insurance*, the Supreme Court held that the guardian should not be partially exonerated in case

368. 2022 SCJ 17.
369. 2021 SCJ 139.
370. 1977 MR 309.
371. 2009 SCJ 52.
372. 1990 MR 9 and 16.

of contributory negligence by the victim.[373] This position is grounded on a strict interpretation of Article 1384 paragraph 6 which only mentions the exclusive fault of a victim.[374]

373. 2021 SCJ 364.
374. *See* para. 161 above.

Chapter 4. Exemption Clauses

210. To our best knowledge, there currently is no case law on the validity of exemption clauses in the field of tort law. This is not surprising as, very often, unlike contractual liability, there is no previous relationship between the tortfeasor and the victim of aharm.[375] French case law, as it is a persuasive authority for the civil law of Mauritius, prohibits such clauses.[376] The solution has been clearly set out for civil liability based on fault, but it is less certain regarding the strict liability regimes.[377] We are of the view that exemption clauses should be generally prohibited in the tort law of Mauritius in order to ensure the efficient prevention of losses in society. In cases where such clauses would be valid, that would certainly entail a lower degree of attention and would increase the number and quantity of losses.

375. *See*, under French law, Porchy-Simon, *supra* n. 131, at 380; Virginie Larribau-Terneyre, *Droit civil. Les obligations* (Sirey, 18th ed. 2022) para. 3045.
376. Porchy-Simon, *supra* n. 131, at 388; Larribau-Terneyre, *supra* n. 376, at para. 3045.
377. Porchy-Simon, *supra* n. 131, at 380–381.

Part V. Causation

211. Even though it is not explicitly mentioned in Articles 1382–1386 Civil Code as a distinct prerequisite, causation is necessarily one of the requirements that has to be met in order to establish civil liability. There needs to be a sufficient causal link between the loss alleged by the claimant and the unlawful act of the defendant. Otherwise, the defendant will not be compensated under the rules of the Mauritian tort law. Causation has to be proved by the person who asserts having suffered harm due to the defendant's unlawful act. This is a natural consequence of one of the core principles governing the civil law of Mauritius, i.e., *actori incumbit probatio*.[378]

212. Causation is a juridical fact (*fait juridique*) and not a juridical act (*acte juridique*), which means that Article 1341 Civil Code does not apply, and claimants have the entire freedom to determine what means of proof they wish to use before a court of justice in order to prove the existence of causation.[379] Thus, they may use written documents, cite the witnesses or use precise and serious evidence (*indices graves, précis et concordants*). In the case *L. Iyemparooma v. CIP Ltée* of 2010,[380] the Intermediate Court of Mauritius held that there were no precise and serious hints that would allow the Court to reach the conclusion that the causation existed. A person had suffered food poisoning and asked the Court to declare the seller liable for his personal harm on the grounds that the bottles of mineral water sold by the seller to that person had not been in good condition and that the food poisoning had been caused by those bottles. Drawing upon all the circumstances of the case, the Court reached the conclusion that it has not been certain enough whether the food poisoning resulted from the consumption of the water or from the traditional home-made dish that the claimant ate a day before he fell sick.

213. There are two possible tests that might be used and have been used to a certain extent by the Supreme Court of Mauritius, namely the 'equivalence of conditions' test and the 'adequate causation' test.

---

378. According to Art. 1315(1) Civil Code, '(a) person who claims performance of an obligation must prove it'.
379. Under Art. 1341(1) Civil Code, juridical acts such as contracts involving more than MUR 5,000 must be evidenced by documents executed before a notary or under private signature. On this rule under French law, *see* in the English language R Patrick Vance, *Writings and Oral Proof in Civilian Jurisdictions: A Theoretical and Historical Perspective* 35 (1975) Louisiana Law Review 745.
380. 2010 INT 178.

Chapter 1. 'Equivalence of Conditions' Test

214. According to the 'equivalence of conditions' test, if in a group of conditions that led to the realisation of the final result, some of them are necessary for the realisation of the final result, those conditions may be considered the cause of the result. However, the conditions that form part of the group of conditions that are not necessary for the realisation of the final result are not considered the cause of the result. Applied to the tort law of Mauritius, that means that an act of the tortfeasor, which forms part of a group of conditions that led to the loss suffered by the victim, must be necessary for the realisation of the harm. Otherwise, it will not be considered the cause of the loss.

215. This has been clearly set out in the case *Beau Plan Sugar Estate v. Pultee* of 1994.[381] After having clearly reminded the contents of the equivalence of conditions test, the Supreme Court stated that in the circumstances of the matter submitted to its attention, there was no causation between the defendant's act and the loss suffered by the direct and the indirect victims. An employer committed a fault by not taking into consideration the medical certificate his employee had submitted to him. It has been argued that the stress suffered by the employee due to the refusal to take into account his medical certificate caused his heart attack and his death several years later. The Supreme Court was of the view that the fault of the employer was not necessary for the heart attack and death of the employee (direct victim) and that the heart attack and death would have happened even in the absence of this event, as some other conditions and events were much more likely to be the cause of this personal harm of the employee. The fault of the employer was, therefore, not the cause of the harm suffered by the deceased employee and his widow.[382]

216. In the case *Caprede v. State of Mauritius* of 2010,[383] the application of the 'equivalence of conditions' test also led to the conclusion that a fault committed by a police officer representing the State of Mauritius was not a necessary condition for the realisation of the harm suffered by the deceased victim and his mother. A person in police custody committed suicide, and it has been established by the Court that a police officer had committed a fault when he did not do the periodic checks of the detainees, as he was supposed to do. However, the Supreme Court was of the view that the fault committed by the police officer had not been the necessary condition for the harm suffered by the detainee and his mother, as the preparation of the suicide does not take much time and the suicide could have been committed even if the police officer had regularly checked on that particular detainee.[384]

381. 1994 SCJ 399.
382. According to the judgment, '(i)n our view, in the light of the evidence, such as it was, it was not reasonable or permissible to infer that the cardiac infarction was due to stress following the refusal of the Appellant to retire the late Mr. Pultee on the medical grounds put forward by Dr. Matabadul. Such an inference would have been too speculative to sustain a causal connection'.
383. 2010 SCJ 147.
384. The Supreme Court held that 'the police officers were no doubt culpable of neglect of duty but the evidence falls short of proving that it is their neglect which caused the detainee to take his own life and for which the defendants should be held responsible'.

Chapter 2. 'Adequate Causation' Test

217. Unlike the 'equivalence of conditions' test, the 'adequate causation' test does not recognise as legal causes all the conditions that have led to the loss. A civil fault that is necessary for the realisation of the harm suffered by the victim may not be recognised as the cause of the harm if that fault is not, in the normal cause of events, able to cause harm. Adequate causation can be described as a positive answer given by a reasonable person to the question: can the defendant's unlawful act, in the normal course of events, be considered the cause of the harm suffered by the claimant? The application of this test excludes all unlawful acts that may exceptionally lead to a harm, even though those faults may be necessary, together with other conditions, for the realisation of the harm suffered by the victim.

218. For instance, when a truck owner hands over the keys of the truck to a drunk person, the former commits a civil fault because a reasonable and careful person would never give the keys of a vehicle to a person who has put himself in a dangerous state. If the drunk driver of the truck causes the accident due to his state of drunkenness and severely hurts a pedestrian, the issue is whether the owner of the truck, who committed a civil fault, may be liable in tort for the harm suffered by the pedestrian.[385] If the equivalence test is applied, the answer will be a positive one because the civil fault of the owner of the truck is a necessary condition for the realisation of the harm suffered by the pedestrian; if the owner of the truck had not handed over the keys to the drunk person, the latter would not have driven the truck and the pedestrian would not have been hurt. However, the answer to the above question is a negative one if the adequacy test is applied: the severe injury of the pedestrian is not a normal consequence of the fault of the truck owner. In other words, in the normal course of events, a pedestrian does not get hurt just because the owner of a truck has handed over the keys thereof to a drunk person.

219. The adequacy test is best illustrated in the case *Parmessur & Ors v. Beeharee & Anor* of 2014.[386] A road accident in which two vehicles were involved occurred. It has been established that the fault of the driver of vehicle A has been the exclusive cause of the accident. However, after the accident, while driver A and driver B were grasping the accident that had just occurred and its consequences, an identified third party stole a few personal objects belonging to the driver of vehicle B. The question was whether the driver of vehicle A could be liable for the material loss (personal objects stolen from the car B). If the equivalence test had been applied, the driver of vehicle A would have been liable in tort, as his fault for the accident with vehicle B is a necessary condition for the larceny suffered by the driver of vehicle B and his material harm. However, the Supreme Court applied the adequacy test in this case and the driver of vehicle A was not held liable. A larceny is an exceptional consequence of a road (car) accident, as most of the time, no personal objects are stolen from the vehicles. This is why the fault of the driver of

385. Cass, Civ 2, 13 Jun. 1974, No. 73-10932.
386. 2014 SCJ 135.

vehicle A who caused the road accident cannot be considered the cause of the larceny suffered by the driver of vehicle B and his material harm. The adequate cause for this harm is, of course, the act of the thief.

Chapter 3. Harm Caused by a Group or by Simultaneous Acts of Two or More Persons

220. It may occur that the harm has been caused by two or more persons acting together in a relatively speaking organised group. For instance, someone in a group of five hunters hunting together has shot a passer-by and it cannot be ascertained which hunter has taken the shot that reached the passer-by. Or, several children playing football together on the street accuse each other of breaking the neighbour's window in a way that makes it impossible to ascertain which child in the group has really broken the window. The question is whether the victim may be awarded reparation under the tort law of Mauritius in both cases.

221. One possibility is to consider that the victim cannot be compensated for his or her harm as it is impossible to link the harm to an act of a specific member of the group. The other solution consists of considering all the members of the group as an entity and declaring all the members of the group liable *in solido* for the harm suffered by the victim. According to this interpretation, causation exists between the act of the group as a whole and the loss suffered.

222. For the time being, the Mauritian Supreme Court applies the first solution set out in the previous paragraph. In the case *Emamally & Ors v. Patun & Anor* of 1975,[387] a passer-by had been killed by one of two hunters having hunted together. It was impossible to determine which hunter exactly shot the passer-by. The Court held that there was no causal link between the act of a specific hunter and the harm suffered by the direct victim and his heirs. No one was held liable in tort.

223. This solution is not favourable to the victim and does not seem consistent with considerations of justice and equity: it is well known that a member of the group has caused harm to the victim, but just because it is not known which specific member of the group did it, the victim is left without compensation. It could be more just and equitable to consider all the members of the group as a whole acting together and to declare all the members of the group liable *in solido*. This would provide excellent protection to the victim. From a technical point of view, this solution may be justified by a common fault committed by the members of the group in the organisation, the execution of their common activity[388] or by the common guardianship of the object that hurt the victim.[389]

224. It also may happen that the authors of the harm may be identified and that they cause harm simultaneously and in two independent actions. For instance, the driver of vehicle A and the driver of vehicle B both commit a civil fault that led to

387. 1975 SCJ 34.
388. Articles 1382–1383 Civil Code. – *See also* under French law Cass, Civ 2, 6 Mar. 1968, Bull Civ II, No. 76.
389. Article 1384 Civil Code. – *See also* under French law Cass Civ 2, 5 Feb. 1960, *D* 1960, 305; 11 Feb. 1966, *D* 1966, 228.

a road accident in which a third party is hurt. In that case, the driver of vehicle A and the driver of vehicle B will be liable in tort *in solido* for the harm suffered by the third party.

225. The liability *in solido* is very protective of the victim of the harm. The latter may choose amongst two or more members of the group or two or more persons having caused the same harm simultaneously and in two or more independent actions, the person against whom the action will be brought before a court and, in that case, the action will certainly be directed against the person who is in the victim's opinion the most financially at ease. The person against whom the action is brought will be obliged to compensate the victim for all the harm suffered and does not have the right to ask the victim to divide his or her claim. Once the defendant has compensated the victim for all his harm, he or she may bring an action against the other members of the group or the other persons having caused the same harm simultaneously and in two or more independent actions and request to be reimbursed for a part of what has been paid to the victim. The amount of that reimbursement will depend on the existence and the gravity of the fault committed by the members of the group or the persons having caused the same harm simultaneously but in two or more independent actions.[390]

390. *See* under French law Cass Civ 2, 5 Jun. 1991, Bull Civ II, No. 175.

Chapter 4. Predispositions of the Victim

226. The issue of the impact of the predispositions of the victim, i.e., of his or her previous health condition, on the existence of the causality link was raised in the case *Parisot v. Emrith* of 1967,[391] where the claimant who had weak nerves had been involved in a road accident and has suffered personal injury, namely a nervous breakdown. The defendant asserted that the personal injury of the victim was due to her predisposition (weak nerves) and could not be linked to the road accident. The Supreme Court rejected this argument as the predisposition of the victim has not entailed any visible incapacity prior to the road accident. In this particular case, the predisposition of the victim did not have any impact on the existence of the causal link.

391. 1967 MR 107.

Part VI. Remedies

Chapter 1. General Principles

227. Under the law of Mauritius, the consequence of civil liability is the obligation to compensate the victim for all the loss suffered. As has been said before, the objective is to place claimants in the position where they were before the harm was caused, i.e., to compensate them for the entire harm. This is known as the principle of full compensation for harm (*principe de la réparation intégrale*), regularly mentioned by the Supreme Court.[392]

392. *See* for example *Cooppen & Anor v. New India Assurance Co Ltd* [2022 SCJ 17]; *Allymamod v. Nujjoo & Anor* [2021 SCJ 139] ('It is nevertheless still incumbent upon the plaintiff to prove each and every particulars of her claim in order to be fully compensated as the principle remains that of the *réparation intégrale*, that is neither a loss nor a profit').

Chapter 2. Kinds of Damages

§1. Individual and Collective Damage

228. In Mauritius, the harm that a victim may be compensated for is necessarily the individual one. The collective harm, such as the harm suffered by all the members of society due to heavy environmental pollution, does not fall within the scope of the Mauritian tort law and might be dealt with by the administrative law.[393]

§2. Direct and Indirect Harm

229. In Mauritius, there can be two types of victims: direct ones (*victimes directes*) and indirect ones (*victimes par ricochet*). The direct victim has suffered direct harm, either moral or material. The indirect victim suffers personal harm caused by the harm suffered by the direct victim. It is obvious that the indirect victim must be close to the direct victim. For instance, a father, a mother, a brother or a sister might suffer material or moral harm in case of death of the direct victim and they qualify as indirect victims. A *fiancé* or a close friend can also suffer material or moral harm when the direct victim is heavily injured.

§3. Pecuniary and Non-pecuniary Losses

230. Under the law of Mauritius, harm can be defined as the violation of a legally protected interest.[394] If the violated interest is property or another economic interest that can be evaluated in money, it is called material loss. In case the violated interest is a non-economic one, such as the reputation of a person or distress due to physical integrity, it is called moral loss.

I. Material Loss (*dommage matériel*)

231. Material loss (*dommage matériel*) is the violation of a legally protected interest that can be evaluated in money. There are three types of material harm, namely economic loss suffered (*perte subie*), missed gain (*gain manqué*) and loss of a chance (*perte d'une chance*).

232. Material loss suffered consists of the decrease in the value of the material wealth of an individual. For instance, an individual will suffer a material loss when an object belonging to him or her and having a commercial value is destroyed or damaged. Medical fees paid because a victim of a road accident needed to stay in

393. *See* para. 183.

394. For French Civil Law as a persuasive authority, *see* for example Romain Ollard, *La distinction du dommage et du préjudice en droit pénal*, Revue de science criminelle et de de droit pénal comparé 2010, 561.

a private clinic for a certain period of time and receive medical assistance is another example of economic loss (*perte subie*). Those medical fees give rise to a decrease in the victim's material wealth.

233. Missed gain is an economic gain on which the victim could have counted if the tortfeasor had not committed the unlawful act. It is an economic gain that is almost certain, given the circumstances of the case. In other words, missed gain is an economic gain that would have been earned by the victim in the normal course of events if the tortfeasor had not committed a civil fault. For instance, if a contract for services between a plumber and his client cannot be executed due to a fault of a driver who has hurt the plumber after the contract has been made and before its execution has commenced, the plumber will be compensated by the driver for all the material harm he has suffered, namely for his missed gain (the payments that he was unable to earn). Another example: if a truck driver, tired and badly concentrated, loses control over the vehicle and destroys the ground floor of a house, its owner will be compensated for all missed gain, namely the rent that the owner was receiving from his tenants. If the truck driver had not committed a civil fault and had not destroyed the ground floor of the house, the owner would have almost certainly continued to receive the rent from his tenants until the end of the tenancy agreement. However, there must be a high degree of certainty that the missed gain would have been earned if the tortfeasor had not committed his civil fault. This is confirmed in the case *Dabee v. Ramtohul of 1967*,[395] where the Supreme Court held that the income that was not certain in the absence of the tortfeasor's fault does not qualify as missed gain. It simply qualifies as hypothetical harm (*dommage hypothétique*).[396]

234. Loss of a chance (*perte d'une chance*) is the third and last form of material harm. First, there has to be a loss of an opportunity to earn a material gain. For instance, if a victim of a car accident is a skilled university student and the accident did not prevent him or her from completing the degree that he or she has been doing at the moment the car accident occurred, the student will not be compensated for loss of an opportunity, as he or she has not lost the opportunity to complete his or her degree and to find a well-remunerated job in the future.[397] Once the opportunity to earn a material gain has been lost, the victim of that loss must prove that the opportunity to earn the material gain had been a serious one. This has been clearly

395. 1967 MR 8.
396. According to the judgment, 'it is not in dispute that a Court may, in suitable cases, award damages for a future prejudice. The rule governing such awards was clearly stated in *Cervello & Ors. v. The Vacoas Transport Co Ltd* [1963 MR 68] where it was held that "prospective prejudice arising from a *délit* or *quasi-délit* may justify present award for damages although such prejudice has not yet accrued if its occurrence is certain to happen as a natural sequel to an existing state of things, provided that its pecuniary assessment is possible." The future *préjudice* must be "*certain et susceptible d'évaluation immédiate.*" It is only when the judge has the "certitude" that the plaintiff will suffer a future prejudice that he may assess the prospective monetary loss. (*See also* Dalloz, Répertoire Pratique, Vo. Responsabilité Civile, N. 256) and following and the decision of the Court of Cassation reported in D. P.1932.1.102 and the report of Mr. Pilon to the Court wherein it is stated that "*un préjudice éventuel ne peut justifier une condamnation actuelle en réparation*"'.
397. Cass. Crim., 10 Jan. 1996, No. 95-80686.

stated by the French Court of Cassation which is a persuasive authority in Mauritius.[398] This type of material harm was addressed in the case dealt with by the Intermediate Court *Calleechurn Ashwin Kumar v. Bhoyro Satteedeo & Ors* of 2007.[399] The loss of a serious opportunity to complete a degree qualifies as a loss of a chance, for which the claimant may be compensated.

235. It has to be noted that the main difference between missed gain and loss of a chance is the degree of certainty. Missed gain is a future gain which is almost certain according to the normal course of events. On the contrary, loss of a chance is a future gain that is highly probable (70 or 80%, for instance), yet not almost certain. This is why, when a court determines the amount of compensation for loss of an opportunity, it will always take into account the degree of the probability that the future economic gain the victim could have actually earned. The amount of the compensation granted to the victim will be proportionate to this probability and will not be equal to the whole gain that could have been earned. For instance, if a party to civil litigation had a serious chance to win the litigation that is estimated by a Judge at 80% and the total gain expected from the litigation is MUR 1,000,000, then the victim who could not continue the litigation due to a civil fault committed by his or her lawyer will be compensated by the latter for MUR 800,000, which is 80% of the total gain that the victim could have expected, had he or she been able to continue the litigation and had he or she won that litigation.

II. Moral Loss (*dommage moral*)

236. Moral harm may be defined as the violation of a legally protected interest that cannot be directly evaluated in money, such as reputation, dignity, etc. Moral harm consists of the victim's suffering, both psychological and physical.

237. Psychological suffering may result from the violation of someone's dignity and reputation. For instance, when a director of a company is revoked, this revocation, which can be freely done by the company, must not be done in an abusive way that hurts the feelings and the reputation of the director.[400] If the revocation of a director has been done in an abusive way, the psychological suffering qualifies as moral harm and the victim will be awarded compensation.[401] Moral harm caused by the violation of someone's dignity and reputation is recognised by the Mauritian

398. *See* for example Cass Civ 1, 21 Nov. 2006, Bull Civ I, No. 498 ('Only the loss of a certain possibility to earn a material gain qualifies as loss of an opportunity.'). However, it needs to be noted that the French Court of Cassation has subsequently abandoned this standpoint and has held that a victim must be awarded compensation even for a small loss of a chance to earn a material gain (e.g., Cass Civ 2, 25 May 2022, No. 20-16351). However, we are of the view that this position should not be followed by the Supreme Court of Mauritius, as it blurs the distinction between a hypothetic harm and a loss of a chance.

399. 2007 INT 63.

400. Cass Com, 26 Apr. 1994, No. 92-15884.

401. Cass Com, 1 Feb. 1994, No. 92-11171.

case law. For example, in the case *La Sentinelle Ltd v. Dayal* of 2000,[402] the Supreme Court held that a local newspaper had insulted the former Commissioner of Police and caused him psychological suffering that qualifies as moral harm. In fact, in one of the newspaper's editions, the journalist put behind the name of the former Commissioner of Police the abbreviation M.A.C.R.O which is a serious insult in the Mauritian Creole language. Moreover, in the case *Police v. Bundhoo Mohamed Ali Dilshad & Anor* of 2007,[403] the Intermediate Court held that even a company, which is a legal entity, has the right to be compensated for moral harm caused by a violation of its dignity and reputation. An employee of the company has forged the exportation visas and when the forgery has been discovered by the US customs, the reputation of the company has been seriously compromised, which led to the compensation of this moral harm.

238. A claimant may also be compensated for his or her loss of the enjoyment of life (*préjudice d'agrément*) which consists of the impossibility for the victim to enjoy the everyday pleasures and activities due to an injury caused by the tortfeasor. This definition was asserted by the French Court of Cassation, sitting in full court: '(l)oss of the enjoyment of life is a subjective harm of personal nature that consists of the troubles felt in the conditions of existence'.[404] This type of loss has been mentioned in the case *Dabee v. Ramtohul* of 1967.[405] Another form of moral harm for which the direct victim can be compensated is disfigurement, i.e., the psychological suffering of the victim due to his or her mutilation or disfigurement.

239. In Mauritius, the direct victim can also be compensated for physical suffering due to the tortfeasor's act. This has been clearly confirmed in the cases *Boodhoo v. Ramsamy & Anor* of 1985,[406] *Mohonee v. New India Assurance Co Ltd* of 2019[407] and *Dabee v. Ramtohul* of 1967.[408] The Intermediate Court adopted the same position in the case *Lal Mahomed Bibi Mymoon v. Mauritius Union Assurance Co Ltd* of 2007.[409]

240. One of the main difficulties and one of the main arguments against the idea of compensation for moral harm is that, while the infringed right (dignity, reputation, physical integrity, etc.) does not have a market value, the compensation consists of a sum of money. This means that, unlike the compensation for material

402. 2000 SCJ 92.
403. 2007 INT 296.
404. Cass Ass plén, 19 Dec. 2003, No. 02-14783. However, it needs to be noted that in France, since 2005, an important part of the loss of the enjoyment of life has been replaced by the notion of lack of functionality (*deficit fonctionnel*). *See* Knetsch, *supra* n. 59, at para. 336.
405. 1967 MR 8.
406. 1985 SCJ 22. In this case, the Supreme Court held that the right to be financially compensated for physical suffering of the direct victim passed to his or her heirs when the direct victim did not pass away right after the accident ('There is authority to say that the plaintiffs, as heirs of the deceased, are entitled to claim damages in respect of the sufferings which the latter suffered before his death').
407. 2019 SCJ 16.
408. 1967 MR 8.
409. 2007 INT 68.

harm, the compensation for moral harm does not reflect the value of the object that has been harmed. It is impossible to evaluate precisely the physical or psychological pain suffered by the direct victim. However, compensation for moral harm is a trite law in Mauritius today. It is deemed that, in spite of the difficulties in assessing the amount of moral harm, it is better to financially compensate the victim of moral harm and ease his or her pain off than to leave this victim without compensation. This has been clearly stated in the case *Boodhoo v. Ramsamy & Anor* of 1985.[410]

241. The indirect victim (*victime par ricochet*) may also be compensated for his or her material harm suffered due to the death or serious injury of the direct victim. First of all, the indirect victim can be awarded this type of compensation when he or she has the right to alimony with the deceased or severely injured direct victim. For instance, Article 203 Civil Code stipulates that the parents have to provide alimony (food, clothes, roof, etc.) to their minor children. In case of death of a parent who was providing alimony to his or her children, the economic loss suffered by the children qualifies as material harm to the indirect victim. More precisely, the harm suffered by the indirect victim is a missed gain because if the direct victim had not been killed by the tortfeasor, the children, in the normal course of events, would have continued to receive financial support (alimony) from the deceased parent. Moreover, under Article 212 Civil Code, a spouse must provide alimony to the other when the latter needs it. Thus, when the spouse who was providing the alimony had been killed in an accident, the tortfeasor will be obliged to compensate the other spouse for the material harm that he or she has suffered: the lost alimony.

242. Compensation for this type of material harm suffered by the indirect victim has been clearly confirmed in the Mauritian case law. In the case *Boodhoo v. Ramsamy & Anor* of 1985,[411] the Supreme Court awarded compensation for their material harm to the wife and three children of the person who died in a car accident. The amount of the compensation has been calculated by multiplying the amount that the direct victim was spending every month on his wife and his children. The same approach was taken in the case *Gokhool v. Groupement français d'assurances* of 2009,[412] where the Supreme Court held that the spouse and two children of the deceased person, six and ten years old, may be compensated for material harm suffered, i.e., the alimony lost that the deceased husband and father was paying to his wife and his children.

243. The case of indirect victims who are not legally bound to the deceased direct victim is more delicate. In other words, can indirect victims who do not have the right to alimony be compensated for the material loss caused by the death of the

410. 1985 SCJ 22. According to this judgment, '(t)he difficulty lies in the assessment of the moral damage suffered by the *de cujus* [the deceased] during the short time he lived after the accident. Any such assessment must necessarily be an arbitrary one. I estimate the damage suffered in the present case at MUR 2,500'.

411. 1985 SCJ 22.

412. 2009 SCJ 412.

direct victim? For the time being, and except for the specific case of unmarried partners, there is no case law in Mauritius that would answer the above question. However, there is an interesting case law of the French Court of Cassation according to which indirect victims who are not linked to the direct victim through the right to alimony may be compensated for their material loss, if they were receiving from the deceased direct victim a regular and voluntary financial aid. In case of death of the direct victim, the loss of the regular and voluntary financial aid qualifies as missed gain, i.e., a financial gain that would have been received in the normal course of events, if the direct victim had not died. For instance, if a grandmother helps financially, on a regular and voluntary basis, her grandchild to which, under Article 203 Civil Code, she does not owe the alimony, then in case of demise of the grandmother, the grandchild will be compensated for the loss of this regular and voluntary financial help.[413] Moreover, if a priest helps financially, on a regular and voluntary basis, a devotee and her daughter, and then the priest dies, the tortfeasor who caused the priest's death will be obliged to compensate the devotee and her daughter for their material harm, i.e., the loss of the financial aid that the priest was providing them with on a regular and voluntary basis.[414]

244. However, there is a well-established case law in Mauritius that an unmarried partner as the indirect victim cannot be compensated for his or her material loss, i.e., the loss of the financial aid that he or she was receiving from the other partner, in case of death of that other partner.

245. The first argument used to justify the refusal to compensate an unmarried partner as an indirect victim is the immorality of the situation of two persons living under the same roof as husband and wife without being legally married. This argument has been put forward by Judge Petrides in the case of *Moutou v. Mauritius Government Railways* of 1933.[415] The second argument used to justify the refusal to compensate an unmarried partner as indirect victim is the lack of legally protected interest (*intérêt juridiquement protégé*). This has been clearly set out in the case *Jugessur & Ors v. Bestel & Anor* of 2007.[416] The third argument used to justify the refusal to compensate an unmarried partner as the indirect victim is some

413. Cass Crim, 2 May 1983, No. 80-95264.
414. Cass Crim, 20 Mar. 1973, No. 72-90866.
415. 1933 MR 102. According to this judgment, 'it is not necessary for the purpose of this "*jugement*" to decide whether that is so, in view of the conclusion I have come to that an action does not lie under Art. 1382 by reason of the termination of a "*pacte immoral*" such as that of "*concubinage*"'.
416. 2007 SCJ 106. According to this judgment, '(i)t appears though from the above note that even in France some reservations are felt by the Courts and the position of the concubine is not the same as that of the widow in such matters', but '(o)ur own country has its own customs; religious marriages hold an important consideration and are recognized by an important sector of the population. To call a woman religiously but not civilly married a concubine is not exactly accurate. It is probably such considerations that have led the legislator to give certain legal effect to religious marriages. (Vide Arts 228-1 to 228-10 of the Code Civil). However, such marriages must be celebrated in accordance with the provisions of the Civil Status Act (Vide ss 26 and 27 of the Civil Status Act). In the case of religious marriages celebrated before the reforms of 1981, such religious marriages may be registered with the Registrar of Civil Status under s. 74 of the Civil Status Act. Unfortunately, the religious marriage of plaintiff no. 1 with the deceased having not been registered

kind of legal fault: 'the parties by their own choice have placed themselves outside the protection which the law offered to them within the marriage bond'. This has been confirmed in the case of *Naikoo v. Société Héritiers Bhogun* of 1972.[417]

246. It is interesting to note that the current case law in Mauritius on the above-analysed legal issue is one of the rare examples where the Mauritian Supreme Court did not follow the legal reasoning expressed in a judgment of the French Court of Cassation. Since the 1970s, the French case law has granted compensation to an unmarried partner for the material harm suffered due to the demise of the other unmarried partner. The unmarried partner may be compensated as the indirect victim for his material loss.[418]

247. It is also to be noted that an indirect victim may also be compensated for his or her moral loss, i.e., for the psychological suffering caused by the death or the invalidity of the direct victim.[419]

248. In case the indirect victim is kin by blood or kin by marriage, there is a presumption that the indirect victim has suffered moral harm due to the demise or the injury of the direct victim. This presumption is a very natural one, as it takes into consideration the reality: most of the time when a person dies or is injured, his or her blood relatives or relatives by marriage will suffer psychologically. This psychological suffering qualifies as moral harm to the indirect victim, and this victim can be compensated for it. The indirect victim does not have to prove, before a court of justice, his psychological suffering and its intensity. The rule has been clearly confirmed in the cases *Gutty & Ors v. Eleonore* of 1980[420] and *Gokhool S D v. Groupement français d'assurances* of 2009.[421]

249. The above-mentioned presumption is not an absolute one; it is a simple one, meaning that it can be overturned, and the tortfeasor will not be obliged to compensate a close blood relative or a relative by marriage for his moral harm caused by the death or injury of the direct victim. For instance, most of the time, a son or a daughter will suffer psychologically in case of death or injury of his or her father or mother. However, there can be exceptions when the personal relation between them so deteriorated, prior to the demise of the direct victim, that the indirect victim could not seriously assert that he or she has suffered moral harm. This reasoning has been confirmed in the case of *Scott v. Brasse* of 1968.[422] A woman who never formally divorced her husband has lived for a long time separated from him and has even started a personal relationship with another man with whom she was sharing the same roof. When her husband died, she asked for compensation for

---

and in the teeth of the authorities that plaintiff no. 1 has to have an *intérêt juridiquement protégé*, I must hold that plaintiff no. 1 is not entitled to any material or moral damages'.

417. 1972 MR 66.
418. Cass Ch mixte, 27 Feb. 1970, No. 68-10276.
419. Cass Civ 2, 1 Jul. 2010, No. 09-15907; 8 Dec. 1971, No. 70-12550.
420. 1980 SCJ 312.
421. 2009 SCJ 412.
422. 1968 MR 31.

her moral harm. The Supreme Court rejected this claim as she could not have suffered psychologically due to the death of her lawful husband from whom she had been separated for a long time.

250. Indirect victims who are not close blood relatives or relatives by marriage of the direct victim may also be compensated for their moral harm, but this time, the moral harm, i.e., the psychological suffering, will not be presumed. A friend or a fiancé of the direct victim will have to prove that his or her feelings for the direct victim were so strong that he or she deserves to be compensated for his or her moral harm.

§4. Pure Economic Loss

251. Pure economic loss, defined as 'financial damage suffered as the result of the negligent act of another party which is not accompanied by any physical damage to a person or property',[423] is not a specific category in the classification of harm under the law of Mauritius. For instance, loss of profit, profitability or some other form of financial gain are part of missed gain and thus reparable losses.

§5. Actual and Future Damage (Lost Profits)

252. As already explained,[424] claimants may be compensated for their missed gain (*gain manqué*), i.e., for their future loss, provided that in the normal course of events, they would have earned this income. It has been reminded in the Intermediate Court case *Fedee v. MSPMPC* of 2013,[425] in which the cases *Dabee v. Ramtohul of 1967*[426] and *Cervello & Ors v. The Vacoas Transport Co Ltd* of 1963[427] are quoted as authorities. The same principle has also been stated in the case *Madhoo v. Porlo Taco Co Ltd & Anor* of 1976.[428]

§6. Mitigation of Damages

253. It is clear that, in the field of contractual liability, there is an obligation for the victim of the inexecution of a contractual obligation to mitigate his or her harm. This has been clearly stated in the cases *Transinvest Engineering and Contracting Ltd v. Iframac Transport Co Ltd and Latour Adrien & Ors* of 1989,[429] *Société S*

423. https://www.lexisnexis.co.uk/legal/commentary/halsburys-laws-of-england/negligence/pure-economic-loss (last visited on 30 Jun. 2024).
424. *See* para. 233 above.
425. 2013 INT 105.
426. 1967 MR 8.
427. 1963 MR 68.
428. 1976 MR 69.
429. 1989 SCJ 123. According to this judgment, 'there is indeed, in law, a duty to mitigate damages. This duty undoubtedly has an impact on the extent of damages which are awarded'.

Sawon et fils et Cie v. The Moka Flacq District Council of 2012[430] and *Scalcione v. The Hong Kong and Shanghai Banking Corporation Limited & Anor* of 2011.[431] However, and to our best knowledge, this duty has not been acknowledged by the Supreme Court for actions in tort. The French legal literature, which is a persuasive authority in Mauritius, seems to be favourable to the duty of the victim of a tort to mitigate his or her harm.[432]

430. 2012 SCJ 394.
431. 2011 SCJ 22.
432. *See* for example Philippe le Tourneau & Matthieu Poumarède, Bonne foi – La bonne foi dans l'exécution du contrat, Répertoire de droit civil, 2019, para. 122.

Chapter 3. Assessment and Compensation of Damages

§1. Objective Versus Subjective

254. In Mauritius, the assessment of the harm suffered by the victim is a mix of objective and subjective elements. The assessment of the material harm is based on the objective criteria as this type of harm is financially assessed. In case of a suffered loss (*perte subie*), a Mauritian court will draw upon the market value of the victim's object that has been destroyed or damaged. The court will take into account the state in which the object had been on the very day it was destroyed or damaged, but it will financially assess the harm by taking into account the market value of that object on the day the assessment is made. As far as missed gain (*gain manqué*) is concerned, its assessment is also objective, as the court will take into account the exact amount of the future financial gain expected by the claimant.[433] Also, and as already explained before,[434] the assessment of the loss of a chance (*perte d'une chance*) is also an objective one: the court will take into account the total amount of the gain expected by the victim and will assess the amount of the loss of an opportunity after having ascertained the probability that the victim had to earn that gain (e.g., 70 or 80%).

255. As previously explained, the assessment of moral harm is highly subjective under the tort law of Mauritius as it is not possible to evaluate precisely the claimant's psychological and physical suffering.[435] The court will have the discretionary power to assess the financial compensation to be awarded for the moral harm suffered by the victim, and it will carefully take into account the specific circumstances of every case brought to his or her attention. For example, this has been clearly stated in the case *Vithilingum S v. Seagull Insurance* of 1999.[436]

§2. Methods of Assessing Damages (Concrete Versus Abstract)

256. As already explained in paragraph 1 of this chapter,[437] the assessment of the material loss suffered is a purely objective one, which means that the personal circumstances of the claimant or the defendant (e.g., the defendant was providing help to the claimant, their economic situation, etc.) are not taken into account. The assessment is based either on the market value of the destroyed or damaged object or on the amount of financial gain expected by the victim.

433. *See* para. 233 above.
434. *See* para. 234 above.
435. *Boodhoo v. Ramsamy & Anor* [1985 SCJ 22].
436. 1999 SCJ 124. According to this judgment, '(a)part from "*le préjudice strictement matériel*" the widow and the child are also entitled to compensation for moral prejudice consisting in "*atteinte aux sentiments d'affection, trouble dans les conditions d'existence*"'. For the assessment of the latter head of loss, the court refers to another case in which 'the fact that the widow would have to assume alone the education of her young children was considered to be a very relevant factor'.
437. *See* para. 254 above.

257. In contrast, the assessment of moral harm is highly subjective under the law of Mauritius, as it is not possible to evaluate precisely the psychological and physical suffering of the victim.[438] The court will have the discretionary power to assess the financial compensation to be awarded for the moral harm suffered by the victim, and it will carefully take into account the specific circumstances of every case brought to its attention. This has been clearly stated in the case of *Vithilingum S v. Seagull Insurance* of 1999.[439]

§3. Equitable Limitation of Damages

258. In principle, the victim of a harm is fully compensated for the harm suffered from the tortfeasor's act. This is known as the principle of full compensation (*principe de la réparation intégrale*) and has been mentioned in the case of *Coopen & Anor v. New India Assurance Co Ltd* of 2022.[440] The principle has also been clearly set out in *Allymamod v. Nujjoo & Anor*: 'It is nevertheless still incumbent upon the plaintiff to prove each and every particulars of her claim in order to be fully compensated as the principle remains that of the *réparation intégrale*, that is neither a loss nor a profit.'[441]

259. A careful analysis of the case law reveals that the Supreme Court follows that principle while assessing the material harm suffered by the spouse and children of the deceased direct victim. The strict application of the principle of full compensation leads to the calculation of the amount of the compensation drawing upon the probable duration of life of the direct victim killed or severely handicapped by the tortfeasor. For instance, if the direct victim had been killed in an accident at the age of 33 and was working on an indeterminate work agreement, the amount of the compensation for the material harm suffered by the spouse should be calculated over the period from the death of the direct victim until his or her retirement (e.g., 27 years = 60 years age of retirement – 33 years age at the moment of death of the direct victim). As far as children are concerned, the amount of the compensation for the material harm suffered by the children should be calculated over the period from the death of the direct victim until the majority of the children (e.g., 13 years = 18 years the age of majority in Mauritius – 5 years age of a child at the moment of death of the direct victim). This method of calculation of the amount of material harm suffered by the spouse and children of the deceased direct victim has been applied in the cases *Gokhool v. Groupement français d'assurances* of 2009[442] and *Boodhoo v. Ramsamy & Anor* of 1985.[443] More recently, the same approach has been taken in the case of *Mojee v. Omnicane Ltd* of 2023,[444] where the spouse of a police officer killed in a road accident has been compensated for the loss of the financial help that

438. *Boodhoo v. Ramsamy & Anor* [1985 SCJ 22].
439. 1999 SCJ 124.
440. 2022 SCJ 17.
441. 2021 SCJ 139.
442. 2009 SCJ 412.
443. 1985 SCJ 22.
444. 2023 SCJ 390.

she could have reasonably expected from her deceased husband between the age the latter had in the moment of his death (32 years) and the age of his probable future retirement (60 years).

§4. Methods of Payment (Lump Sum Versus Annuities)

260. Most of the time, the courts will grant a lump sum to the victim of a harm in order to award compensation. For instance, in the case of *Boodhoo v. Ramsamy & Anor* of 1985,[445] the Court has awarded to the claimant a total sum of MUR 280,806. In the case of *Vithilingum v. Seagull Insurance* of 1999,[446] it has been reminded that the appellate court in the case of *New Light Match Co* approved of the approach of the judge in *Kassory & Ors v. Rose Belle SE & Ors* of 1990,[447] where the court granted to a widow moral damages in the sum of MUR 75,000. A lump sum has also been granted to the claimants in the case of *Ramoly & Anor v. Mauritian Eagle Insurance Co Ltd* of 2015.[448] However, nothing prevents the court from ordering the tortfeasor to pay annuities to the victim.

445. 1985 SCJ 22.
446. 1999 SCJ 124.
447. 1990 SCJ 107.
448. 2015 SCJ 196.

Chapter 4. Personal Injury and Death

261. Personal injury and death are not an autonomous form of loss under the law of Mauritius. It is absorbed by the recognised forms of harm, such as suffered harm (*perte subie*), missed gain (*gain manqué*) and loss of a chance (*perte d'une chance*), on the one hand, and moral harm, on the other hand.

§1. Pecuniary Losses

262. Pecuniary losses derived from a personal injury and death may take the form of a suffered harm (*perte subie*), missed gain (*gain manqué*) and loss of a chance (*perte d'une chance*). For instance, when an individual is severely injured in a car accident and needs to be treated in a private medical institution, the medical fees that have to be paid qualify as loss suffered. Moreover, all lost income of the injured person qualifies as missed gain. In cases where the injured person has lost a serious opportunity to earn a financial gain, this qualifies as the loss of a chance. It has been clearly stated in the case of *Seebaru & Anor v. Swan General Ltd* of 2022,[449] where the victim has been compensated for the destruction of his mobile phone, his watch, his laptop, etc., but also for his medical fees and for the missed gain (loss of income). Also, in the case of *Cooppen & Anor v. New India Assurance Co Ltd* of 2022,[450] the Supreme Court reminded that 'the Judicial Committee of the Privy Council set out the different heads under which damages may be awarded for personal injury'.[451]

§2. Non-pecuniary Losses

263. In case of a severe personal injury, claimants may ask for compensation for their psychological suffering due to the disfigurement or to the impossibility of carrying out an activity carried out before. The injured person may also ask for compensation for his or her physical suffering. This has been clearly confirmed in the

449. 2022 SCJ 337.

450. 2022 SCJ 17.

451. *Patel & Ors v. A Beenessreesingh and SICOM Ltd* [2012] UKPC 18. According to this judgment, '(d)amages for personal injury are likely to fall under one or more of four main heads, each of which will need, in the generality of cases, to be separately considered and quantified. They are (i) material (i.e., pecuniary) damage in respect of (a) expenditure occasioned by the injury up to the date of judgement, (b) future costs of care and treatment and (c) loss of earnings both before and after judgement; (ii) moral damages, representing physical and mental suffering, loss of amenity, and, more generally, what the Court de Cassation has recently called "loss of quality of life and of its normal pleasures"'.

case *Seebaru & Anor v. Swan General Ltd* of 2022[452] (disfigurement, impotency, other pain and suffering). As highlighted in the same case, indirect victims may also be compensated for their personal prejudice.[453]

---

452. 2022 SCJ 337.
453. 2022 SCJ 337. According to this judgment, '(i)n *New Light Match Manufacturing Co Ltd v. Mrs WW M. L. Ono & Others* [1990 MR 164], Lallah SPJ and Ahnee J considered the "*préjudice moral (atteinte aux sentiments d'affection, trouble dans les conditions d'existence*" mentioned in Max Le Roy's work, L'Évaluation du Préjudice Corporel, 7e Edition, published in 1977 by Librairies Techniques, Librairie de la Cour de Cassation, at paras 185, 186, 188, 189 and 194, with regard to "*le conjoint de la victime*". It was held that such damages had to be "realistic". I have thus considered that in *Leong Son WW M. & Others v. ENL Limited* [2021 SCJ 242], awards of MUR 1 million and MUR 500,000 were respectively made for the wife and children of the deceased'.

Chapter 5. Various Damages (Property)

264. As already explained in detail in Chapter 2,[454] any destruction or damage of property qualifies in Mauritius as suffered harm (*perte subie*).

454. *See* paras 228–235 above.

Chapter 6. Interference with Collateral Benefits

265. The material harm suffered must be real. In other words, it has a negative impact on the level of the victim's economic wealth. In cases where claimants are entitled to an insurance or a social insurance allowance, they will not be compensated for the part of the loss already covered by the insurance or social security.

266. However, the victim will be entitled to bring an action before a court of justice and to seek compensation against the tortfeasor for the harm that has not been covered by the insurance contract. This has been clearly stated in the case of *Seebaru R. & Anor v. Swan General Ltd* of 2022 and *Soondron L. & Anor v. Swan Insurance Co Ltd & Anor* of 2004.[455]

267. Regarding social security and the compensation of the victim for his or her material harm, sections 5–7 of the National Pension Act of 1976[456] providing for an orphan's pension and a child's allowance are noteworthy. It is very clear that those social security allowances cover a part of the material harm suffered by the indirect victims, that is, the surviving spouse and the children. However, there is no provision in the law of Mauritius that prevents them from claiming, before a court, an amount that will compensate for the difference between the prejudice that they really suffered and the amount received from the social security.

268. Of course, nothing in Mauritian laws will prevent the insurance or the social security from any action in reimbursement brought before a court of justice against the tortfeasor. Thus, according to Article 1983-50 Civil Code, where the insurer compensates his insured, the victim of material harm, the former will automatically enter into all the rights and actions of the latter which means that the insurer will have all the rights and actions that his insured, the victim of the material harm had against the tortfeasor. This has been clearly confirmed in the case *Soondron & Anor v. Swan Insurance Co Ltd & Anor* of 2004.[457] However, Article 1983-50 Civil Code also adds that the above-mentioned subrogation will not apply against the children, ascendants, descendants, relatives by marriage, agents of the insured, and generally against every person living under the same roof with the insured, except where a malicious act would be committed by one of the above-mentioned persons.

455. 2004 SCJ 125. According to this judgment, '(i)n view of the fact that no "cumul" exists in relation to material damages, the plaintiffs are entitled to be compensated by the second defendant for the difference between the actual damages suffered by them and the amount which they have received under their policy of insurance'.

456. Act 44/1976.

457. 2004 SCJ 125.

Chapter 7. Other Remedies

§1. Injunctive Relief

269. Injunctive relief may be defined as a procedural tool that 'restrains a party from doing certain acts or requires a party to act in a certain way'.[458] This measure aims at preventing irreparable harm to the applicant. The grant of injunctive relief may be appealed against and will be reviewed by an appellate court on the grounds of abuse of discretion. The injunctive relief will be cancelled when the appellate court is of the view that the relief has been based on a misapplication of the law or an erroneous factual finding.[459]

270. The conditions for injunctive relief are: (1) irreparable harm for the applicant if the injunction is not made by the Court; (2) the potential harm for the applicant outweighs the harm for the defendant if the injunction is made; (3) the injunction is not hurting public interest; and (4) the applicant has a substantial likelihood of success on the merits.

271. This legal mechanism is not unknown in Mauritius. In the case *Gobin & Anor v. Ramdhony* of 2021,[460] the Intermediate Court stated that '(t)he defendant admitted having on or about 15 September 2016 given an undertaking before the Judge in Chambers, following injunction proceedings lodged against him by the plaintiffs, not to obstruct the exit road. He further admitted having himself removed the offending structures whilst the injunction proceedings were still pending before the Judge'. Injunctive relief has also been mentioned in the case of *Seeboruth v. SBM & Anor* of 2021.[461]

§2. Punitive Damages

272. As the principle of full compensation (*principe de la réparation intégrale*) has been clearly announced in the cases of *Cooppen & Anor v. New India Assurance Co Ltd* of 2022[462] and *Allymamod v. Nujjoo & Anor* of 2021,[463] no punitive damages can be awarded to the claimant. Claimants can only be compensated for their real loss, whereas the punitive damages that do not reflect the real loss suffered would lead to an unjustified enrichment (*enrichissement sans cause*) of the claimant.

458. https://www.law.cornell.edu/wex/injunctive_relief (last visited on 30 Jun. 2024).
459. https://www.law.cornell.edu/wex/injunctive_relief (last visited on 30 Jun. 2024).
460. 2021 INT 136.
461. 2021 INT 35.
462. 2022 SCJ 17.
463. 2021 SCJ 139.

Selected Bibliography

General Works on the Law of Mauritius

Anthony Angelo, *Mauritius: The Basis of the Legal System*, 3 Comparative and International Law Journal of South Africa 228–241 (1970).

Michael Bogdan, *The Law of Mauritius and Seychelles* (Jurisrörlaget i Lund 1989).

Collectif, *Le droit de l'Île Maurice* (LGDJ 2022, coll Bibliothèque de l'Association Henri Capitant).

Pierre Rosario Domingue, *The Historical Development of the Mixed Legal System of Mauritius During the French and British Colonial Periods*, 4 Research Journal of the University of Mauritius 61–93, 95–117 (2002).

Rajendra Gunputh, *Étude sur les justifications et enjeux de la codification dans la tradition de common law : le cas de l'Ile Maurice, pays du commonwealth*, Revue de la recherche juridique 2006, 1694–1721

Jonas Knetsch, *Bibliographie juridique de l'océan Indien/ Legal Bibliography of the Indian Ocean* (LexOI 2021) 131–199.

Jonas Knetsch, *Le métissage juridique dans deux 'petits États' de l'océan Indien : Maurice et les Seychelles*, Comparative Law Journal of the Pacific/Journal de Droit Comparé du Pacifique 2019, special issue, 195–211.

Raymond d'Unienville, *L'évolution du droit civil à l'île Maurice 1721–1968* (Best Graphics 1994, reprint Temple Law Books 2012).

Louis Venchard, *L'application du droit mixte à l'île Maurice*, Mauritius Law Review 1982, no. 4, 29–44.

Legal Sources of Mauritius on the Internet

Government (official website with an index to legislation)
http://www.govmu.org/

Law Reform Commission (official website)
http://lrc.govmu.org

National Assembly (official website)
https://mauritiusassembly.govmu.org/

Supreme Court (official website with a comprehensive database of legislation and case law)
https://supremecourt.govmu.org/

Selected Bibliography

General Works on the Tort Law of Mauritius

Goran Georgijevic, *Mauritian Tort Law*, 68 Anali Pravnog fakulteta u Beogradu 184–203 (2020).

Jonas Knetsch, *La réception du droit français de la responsabilité à Maurice*, Revue internationale de droit comparé 2017, 67–87.

Law Reform Commission, *Discussion Paper: Reform of Law on Responsabilité Civile in the Code Civil Mauricien* (Law Reform Commission 2017).

Jean-Baptiste Seube, *La responsabilité civile*, *in* Collectif, Le droit de l'Île Maurice (LGDJ 2022) 81–88.

General Introduction and Part I

Georges Babinet, *De la responsabilité de l'administration du fait de ses préposés à l'Île Maurice*, Revue juridique et politique. Indépendance et coopération 1973, 885–894.

Goran Georgijevic, *La responsabilité civile des médecins employés par des hôpitaux publics à Maurice*, Revue de droit international et de droit comparé, 2021, no. 4, pp. 519–545.

Jonas Knetsch, *Le principe de 'non-cumul 'entre la responsabilité contractuelle et délictuelle en droit mauricien. Commentaire de l'arrêt Mediterranean Shipping Company v. Sotramon Ltd* [2017] UKPC 23, The New Bar Chronicle 2018, no. 6, 24–27.

Jean-Baptiste Seube, *Responsabilité contractuelle et délictuelle à l'Île Maurice*, IJLS Law Journal 2019, no. 9.

Maurice Rault, *La responsabilité de l'État du fait de ses préposés en droit mauricien*, Revue juridique et politique. Indépendance et coopération 1973, 873–884.

Parts II and III

Éric Agostini, *Responsabilité du fait des choses – L'Île Maurice est encore l'Isle de France*, in *Mélanges Christian Mouly* (Litec 1998, vol. 2) 3–11.

Anthony Angelo, *The Mauritius Approach to Article 1384 of the French Civil Code*, 4 Comparative & International Law Journal of South Africa 57–71 (1971).

Anthony Angelo, *Article 1384 (1) of the Mauritius Civil Code. The continuing story*, 13 Comparative & International Law Journal of South Africa 204–211 (1980).

Satyabhooshun G Domah, *Une analyse des droits français, anglaise et mauricien de responsabilité du fait des choses*, thesis Aix-Marseille 3, 1979.

Goran Georgijevic, *L'entrepreneuriat, le développement durable et la responsabilité délictuelle. Droit mauricien*, Revue juridique de l'environnement 2013, 433–447.

Bernard Parisot, *La jurisprudence mauricienne et la responsabilité du fait des choses*, 5 Cahiers du Centre universitaire de La Réunion 82–97 (1975).

Ariranga G Pillay, *Product Liability in Mauritius*, Mauritius Law Review 1977, no. 1, 45–58.

Part IV

Law Reform Commission, *Issue Paper: Law of Prescription under Code Civil Mauricien* (Law Reform Commission 2013).

Parts V and VI

Goran Georgijevic, *La réparation des préjudices par ricochet du concubin en droit mauricien*, Carnets de recherche de l'océan Indien 2019, no. 4.

Sources of French Civil Law given as persuasive authority in Mauritius

Pascal Ancel, *Droit des obligations en 12 thèmes* (Dalloz, 2nd ed. 2020).
Philippe Brun, *Responsabilité civile extracontractuelle* (LexisNexis, 6th ed. 2023)
Rémy Cabrillac, *Droit des obligations* (Dalloz, 14th ed. 2020).
Emmanuel Dockès, Gilles Auzero & Dirk Baugard, *Droit du travail 2022* (Dalloz, 35th ed. 2021).
Jacques Flour, Jean-Luc Aubert & Éric Savaux, *Droit civil – Les obligations*, vol. 2 *Le fait juridique* (Sirey, 14th ed. 2011).
Jonas Knetsch, *Tort Law of France* (Wolters Kluwer 2021).
Virginie Larribau-Terneyre, *Droit civil – Les obligations* (Sirey, 18th ed. 2022).
Philippe le Tourneau (ed.), *Droit de la responsabilité et des contrats: Régimes d'indemnisation 2023–2024* (Dalloz, 13th ed. 2023)
Philippe le Tourneau & Matthieu Poumarède, *Répertoire de droit civil – Bonne foi – La bonne foi dans l'exécution du contrat* (Dalloz 2019).
Romain Ollard, *La distinction du dommage et du préjudice en droit pénal*, Revue de science criminelle et de droit pénal comparé 2010, 561–585.
Stéphanie Porchy-Simon, *Droit des obligations 2024* (Dalloz, 16th ed. 2023).
René Savatier, *Traité de la responsabilité civile en droit français* (LGDJ, 2nd ed 1951).
François Terré, Philippe Simler, Yves Lequette & François Chénedé, *Droit civil – Les obligations* (Dalloz, 12th ed. 2019).
Geneviève Viney, *Introduction à la responsabilité* (LGDJ, 4th ed. 2019)
Geneviève Viney, Patrice Jourdain & Suzanne Carval, *Conditions de la responsabilité* (LGDJ, 4th ed. 2013)
Geneviève Viney, Patrice Jourdain & Suzanne Carval, *Les régimes spéciaux et l'assurance de responsabilité* (LGDJ, 4th ed. 2017)

Selected Bibliography

Index

The numbers here refer to paragraph numbers.

Index

Index

www.ingramcontent.com/pod-product-compliance
Lightning Source LLC
Chambersburg PA
CBHW070253030525
26096CB00033B/1387